IMAGES OF WAR

THE BATTLE FOR ARNHEM
1944–1945

Allied paratroops being dropped over the Netherlands on 17 September 1944, heralding Operation Market Garden. This was the largest airborne operation since D-Day.

IMAGES OF WAR

THE BATTLE FOR ARNHEM 1944–1945

RARE PHOTOGRAPHS FROM WARTIME ARCHIVES

Anthony Tucker-Jones

Pen & Sword
MILITARY

First published in Great Britain in 2019 by
PEN & SWORD MILITARY
an imprint of
Pen & Sword Books Ltd,
47 Church Street,
Barnsley,
South Yorkshire
S70 2AS

Every effort has been made to trace the copyright of all the photographs.
If there are unintentional omissions, please contact the publisher in writing, who
will correct all subsequent editions.

A CIP record for this book is available from the British Library.

ISBN 978 1 52673 001 5

Typeset by CHIC GRAPHICS

Printed and bound by CPI Group (UK) Ltd, Croydon, CR0 4YY

Pen & Sword Books Ltd incorporates the imprints of Pen & Sword Archaeology,
Atlas, Aviation, Battleground, Discovery, Family History, History, Maritime, Military,
Naval, Politics, Railways, Select, Social History, Transport, True Crime, Claymore
Press, Frontline Books, Leo Cooper, Praetorian Press, Remember When, Seaforth
Publishing and Wharncliffe.

For a complete list of Pen & Sword titles please contact
Pen & Sword Books Limited
47 Church Street, Barnsley, South Yorkshire, S70 2AS, England
E-mail: enquiries@pen-and-sword.co.uk
Website: www.pen-and-sword.co.uk

Contents

Introduction

Operation Market Garden: Eindhoven, Nijmegen and Arnhem, 17 September 1944, three para drops and one armoured charge. It is the stuff of Hollywood and indeed became a film. In theory the airborne forces were to be supported by three whole British corps, but in reality the ground force going to the rescue of the airborne troops amounted to a single corps fighting on a very restricted frontage. At every turn along the route and around Arnhem the Allies were amazed and dismayed at the tenacity shown by the Germans. While they may not have expected a pushover, they were certainly not anticipating what happened.

Under Operation Market British and American parachutists and glider-borne troops landed in the German-occupied Netherlands; at the same time, under Operation Garden, conducted by General Horrocks's British 30th Corps, tanks spearheaded a sixty-mile dash along 'Hell's Highway' to link up with the lightly armed and heavily outnumbered airborne forces. The prize was the last bridge at Arnhem over the Neder Rijn (Dutch Nether Rhine). Taken intact it would provide the Allies with a back door into Germany – the famous '*A Bridge Too Far*'.

After the Allied breakout from Normandy and the sweep to the Seine, Arnhem provided another opportunity for a highly mobile operation that would also hasten the end of the war. The Allied airborne commanders were champing at the bit to have another go, and letting their divisions help Allied tanks leapfrog through the Netherlands seemed tailor-made for their capabilities.

There was only one major snag. In order to prevent the Germans recovering from their defeat in Normandy, the drive to Arnhem had to be conducted as quickly as possible. Therein lay its fatal flaw. Whereas Operation Overlord or D-Day had been the results of months and months of meticulous planning, Market Garden was put together in a matter of a week. It was a daring but appallingly ill-conceived operation. Objections and warnings were simply swept aside. The Allies were intoxicated by the liberation of Paris, and after all the operational bickering in Normandy Field Marshal Montgomery saw a chance to rehabilitate his battered reputation.

Montgomery had been particularly stung by American criticism that he played safe in Normandy. He had been hurt by complaints about his continued failure to capture Caen and break out on the Allied left flank. Montgomery claimed his plan had always been to draw the panzers to Caen, so that the less experienced Americans would have time to take the vital port of Cherbourg and then swing south-east to break out. Privately, though, he must have hoped that his constant attacks on German defences would pay dividends. They did, but not for him: his reputation, forged in North Africa against Rommel, was tarnished. Montgomery knew that if he did something dramatic in September 1944 this would not only speed up the end of the war, but also restore his standing as a general.

In part Montgomery's optimism was based on a contempt for the German fighting soldier. After the Battle of Normandy, he assumed the German armed forces would be unable to resist his headlong charge. There was also a wilful ignoring of inconvenient intelligence. The Allies knew that the 2nd SS Panzer Corps was recuperating in the Arnhem area, but were adamant that it had fewer than 6,000 men and fifty operational tanks and therefore was not up to much. This intelligence assessment proved woefully inadequate, and to make matters worse the paras of the British 1st Airborne Division were not warned that they were dropping on to the SS. The SS, while they may have been exhausted and lacking equipment, were tough veterans who knew how to fight.

While Montgomery was culpable of dismissing the presence of German tanks, his worst mistake was to underestimate German initiative. He should have known from his experiences in North Africa, Italy and Normandy that the Germans were masters of putting together ad hoc battle groups that could fight very effectively. They were often formed using men from disparate units, on occasion rear echelon personnel such as clerks, cooks and drivers, but led by competent non-commissioned officers and junior officers, these battle groups often performed miracles.

The only occasion that the Allies played the Germans at their own game was at Bastogne during the Battle of the Bulge when the Americans threw every available man into the line to prevent a German breakthrough. Montgomery had regularly fought the SS in Normandy and knew what they were capable of, but when it came to Market Garden he simply threw all caution to the wind.

Like most historians, my first exposure to the battle was through Cornelius Ryan's excellent book *A Bridge Too Far* and the subsequent movie based on it. While the latter was marred by the distractions of too many cameos by star actors, it did capture the chaotic nature of the battle. Before *A Bridge Too Far* appeared, Operation Market Garden had been presented as little more than an unfortunate setback following the Allies' triumph in Normandy. Afterwards however, what caught the public imagination was the desperate race against time to reach 1st Airborne, and the division's heroic defence at Arnhem until finally withdrawn. American success at Eindhoven and Nijmegen regrettably became immaterial to Montgomery's overall failure to get over the Rhine. Rather unfairly, General Horrocks's 30th Corps were labelled the villains as their advance had been simply too slow.

Furthermore, as the years rolled by it became very apparent that it was the failure at Arnhem that consigned the Allies to Eisenhower's 'broad front' strategy, which saw the Allies battering themselves against the full length of German defences across Europe. Ironically, although the Germans were steadily driven back, it was they who seized back the strategic initiative by launching the Battle of the Bulge in the winter of 1944, just three months after Arnhem.

The aim of this *Images of War* book is to offer the reader not only a visual introduction to the key battles fought during Operation Market Garden, but also a brief overview of why it failed. Photographs of the Battle for Arnhem are now almost as iconic as those of the Battle of the Bulge. Most titles tend to concentrate on the struggle at Arnhem and nearby Oosterbeek, involving the heroic efforts of British 1st Air Borne Division. This volume is designed to put that element of the battle in its wider context.

* * *

Photograph Sources

All images are from the author's photographic collection.

Notably, the British 1st Airborne Division took a small camera team with them to record their exploits up close and personal. Inevitably many of the pictures taken were to some extent posed for during lulls in the fighting. They were, however, shot under actual combat conditions and this does not detract from their quality. The Germans also took the opportunity to photograph captured British airborne forces. These collective images proved to be iconic and helped define perceptions of the battle.

Many of the British prisoners of war managed to look defiant, even in the face of defeat and gloating Nazi propaganda cameramen. Interpreting photos is always about the finer details. Without wishing to sound flippant, what is particularly striking about the British PoWs are their very modern-looking haircuts. Far from having crewcuts, most looked quite stylish and would not have been out of place on a movie set. The progress of 30th Corps was also recorded visually, most memorably rumbling over Nijmegen road bridge.

Acknowledgements

My thanks to the unsung but highly supportive team at Pen & Sword: commissioning editor Rupert Harding, author liaison Katie Eaton and copyeditor Susan Last. I am also extremely grateful to the late Jean Norman for permitting me to use her husband Alfred's photos of his time with the 53rd (Welsh) Infantry Division.

Chapter One

Monty's Garden

On paper at least, Operation Market Garden looked a major undertaking involving almost a dozen Allied divisions. The ground forces comprised General O'Connor's 8th, Ritchie's 12th and Horrocks's 30th Corps, totalling eight divisions, of which three were armoured. However, it fell to just Horrocks's forces to fight their way up a single road to reach Arnhem while the other corps defended his flanks. This greatly reduced the actual punch of the ground assault.

Lieutenant General Brian Horrocks initially recalled, with some enthusiasm:

On 11th September [1944] I received orders for the advance to Arnhem and realised that once again 30th Corps was to play a leading role. The outline plan was for the 2nd British Army to advance approximately seventy miles to seize the Grave-Nijmegen-Arnhem area and then penetrate still further northwards to the Zuider Zee in order to cut off all the enemy forces in the Low Countries from those in Germany. It was an exciting prospect because, if successful, it would go far to end the war as we should then be in an excellent position from which to outflank the Ruhr.

During his meeting with Field Marshal Bernard Montgomery the following day, at a forward airfield near the small Belgian town of Bourg-Léopold, Horrocks recalled that he was not given detailed orders, but rather briefed on an outline plan. Montgomery was convinced the German Army was still very disorganized after Normandy, and was heading for home as fast as it could go. The start date, or D-Day, for Market Garden was 17 September 1944.

Horrocks's job was to go away, with just five days to spare, and draw up his own 'detailed orders' for 30th Corps, which then had to be approved by Lieutenant General Miles Dempsey, commander of the British 2nd Army. For Horrocks Arnhem would be a tactical battle – that was, after all, the role of a corps rather than an army headquarters.

Horrocks's 30th Corps, which had led the race to Antwerp and Brussels, consisted of the Guards' Armoured Division, the 43rd and 50th Infantry Divisions,

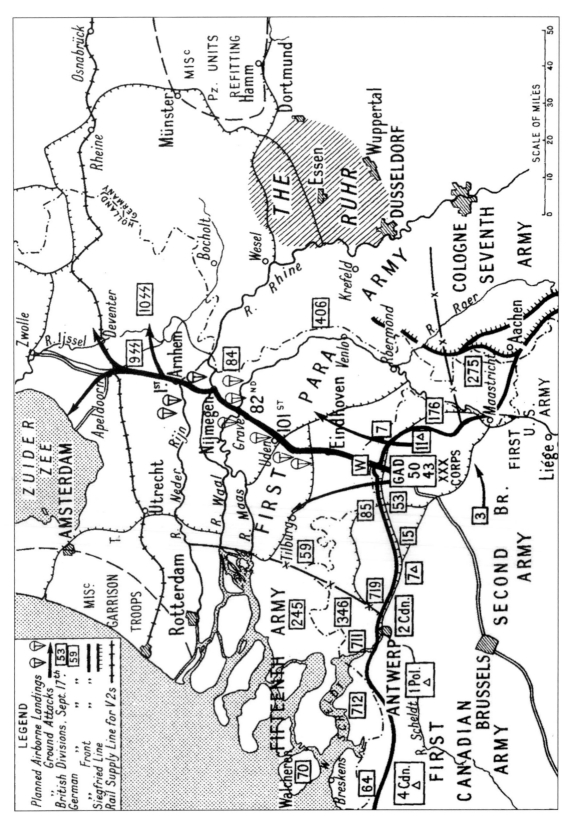

Operation Market Garden: The Plan

8th Armoured Brigade and a Dutch Brigade. They were to break out of their existing bridgehead over the Meuse-Escaut Canal and rumble up the road through Eindhoven, Grave and Nijmegen, which were to be seized by the supporting airborne troops, and on to Arnhem. Horrocks was told that a 'carpet' of some 30,000 airborne troops would be dropped in front of 30th Corps. 'It was a comforting thought,' noted Horrocks. The only problem was that the term 'carpet' seemed to imply some sort of passive role for the airborne divisions.

Although it all sounded so simple, from the start Horrocks had his reservations. Between him and Arnhem flowed not only the immense Meuse (or Maas), Waal and Lower Rhine (Neder Rijin) rivers, but also three wide canals, which would have to be crossed first. His intelligence showed that all the bridges had been prepared for demolition by the Germans. If the paratroops failed to grab them intact, British engineers would have to bring up Bailey bridges. This would take time, and that was something Horrocks did not have. Aerial photo reconnaissance was conducted of all the bridges so that the engineers would know exactly what to expect at each location. In the Bourg-Léopold area Montgomery gathered 9,000 engineers with 2,300 vehicles and all their bridging equipment. Horrocks's 30th Corps had a total of 20,000 vehicles.

The local Dutch terrain was not ideal for Horrocks's tanks, as it was a combination of marsh and woodland. This meant his men would be unable to carry out all-important flanking operations to clear German defences. When he examined the maps of his route, to his horror he realised they could only advance up a single road – Highway 69. If this became blocked it would throw out his timetable, and if any of the bridges were blown it would take forever to get the engineers forward.

Horrocks and his commanders resolved to use the road like a railway. Traffic would be strictly scheduled, and their men would have to carry as much ammunition, food and petrol as they could. As they fought their way forward, traffic control posts and breakdown teams were to be established behind them. Nothing must block the route: any disabled vehicles would be simply shunted into the verges.

'The only thing I could do was blast my way down the main road on a comparatively narrow front with as much air and artillery support as I could get,' said Horrocks. This would not be easy. He was well aware that the Germans were constantly reinforcing their forces in front of him. Even if Horrocks pierced the German defences, he knew that the local waterways would still impede him.

Despite all these problems, Horrocks was not despondent about the challenge facing him. A commander's job is to problem-solve, not complain. 'In spite of these difficulties, however,' wrote Horrocks, 'I was confident that we should win through. The troops were in great heart. I had an experienced and very able staff, and the end of the war seemed to be rapidly approaching.' His latter remark perhaps indicated a certain unhealthy complacency about the German will to fight.

On 16 September Horrocks summoned his commanders to the cinema in Bourg-Léopold to issue orders. At 1030 hours he took to the stage 'in a high-necked woolly with a battledress top and a camouflaged airborne smock.' Looking round the room he saw the familiar faces of men with whom he had fought side-by-side since El Alamein. Horrocks had learned from Montgomery that orders should be simple, clear and concise.

He explained how weak the enemy was, and the different roles of the Market airborne forces and the Garden ground forces. While the audience digested this, Horrocks added that speed was essential: 'we must reach the lightly equipped 1st British Airborne Division if possible in forty-eight hours'. Optimistically it was hoped that if the bridges were captured undamaged, the leading elements of 30th Corps could reach Arnhem within twenty-four hours.

Horrocks did not record any reaction to this piece of news, but his officers must have silently wondered if they could get to the paras in just two days. It seemed at best a fairly optimistic timetable – thirty miles a day. Perhaps their massed artillery and the RAF's fighter-bombers would blast the enemy out of the way; but then again perhaps not. It seemed a gamble. He continued:

> As soon as a report is received of any demolition the road will be cleared of all traffic and the Royal Engineers unit earmarked for this particular bridge will be rushed up along what I hope will be a completely open road.

All well and good, thought his officers, but what would the Germans be doing while all this was going on?

Horrocks also warned everyone that as 30th Corps had been given most of the resources, the advance of 8th Corps on the right and 12th Corps on the left would be much slower. Looking at his officers, he said 'we shall be on our own, possibly for quite a long period'. If that were the case it meant, depending on what troops the Germans could muster, that the flanks of 30th Corps would be left wide open to counterattack, without much prospect of protection. The assumption seemed to be that the Germans would be going in the opposite direction, not counterattacking.

Logistics support for the Allies was a challenge, because they had not secured the Channel ports as quickly as hoped. For a long time they were reliant on the badly damaged Cherbourg harbour and the artificial Mulberry harbour off Arromanches for landing supplies. In addition, just before D-Day the Allies had destroyed much of the French railway system as part of Operation Pointblank. This situation led to the creation of the Red Ball Express, which was a truck convoy service that came into being at the end of August 1944 to keep the advancing Allied armies replenished. The supply routes ran from Cherbourg and Arromanches and employed around 6,000 trucks delivering 12,500 tons of supplies a day – a major undertaking.

The Red Ball Express ran for just over 80 days and ended in November 1944 once Antwerp became available to the Allies and enough railways had been repaired. It took drive to get the whole thing going and to keep it moving. Colonel Loren Ayers, who was in charge, was dubbed 'little Patton', which gives some measure of the man. Drivers often removed the engine regulators to increase the speed above the trucks' normal 56kph. The name of the convoy was derived from an old American term for priority cargo on the railways and trains that was marked with a red ball.

Operating the convoy was a very dangerous job, because there was always the risk of mines, German troops left behind the lines, and being strafed by the Luftwaffe. Crashes and pile-ups were not uncommon. The Red Ball Express was operated by non-combat personnel. African-American troops were not typically used in fighting roles, so usually got all the support jobs – in the case of the Red Ball Express they made up two-thirds of the drivers. The troops battling their way across Europe viewed the supply trucks as a godsend: without them the fighting would have simply ground to a halt. Denied the use of Antwerp, Operation Market Garden was reliant on it.

One might question why Horrocks issued his orders just a day before the operation was due to start. It hardly seemed enough time for everyone to prepare. Horrocks argued that he did this to ensure operational security, and because much of the preparatory work had already been done in terms of gathering supplies, positioning artillery and ensuring the Royal Engineers knew what to do. 'There were surprisingly few questions at the end of the orders,' wrote Horrocks, 'though I must say the audience looked very thoughtful as they left the cinema – particularly the Irish Guards'.

General 'Freddie' de Guingand, Montgomery's highly able chief of staff, was not available to help either Dempsey or Horrocks draw up their plans:

> I had unfortunately been away sick in England during most of the period of preparation and only arrived back on the afternoon of the 17th. So I was not in close touch with the existing situation. It was undoubtedly a gamble, but there was a very good dividend to be reaped if it came off. Horrocks was an ideal commander for the task, and morale of the troops was high.

It was evident that Montgomery's headquarters seemed to view the whole thing as a bit of 'a walk in the park'.

German paratroops killed during the battle for Normandy. The abandoned vehicle looks to be an amphibious Schimmwagen, ideal for navigating Europe's rivers. Allied commanders assumed that once the German armed forces had been driven east of the River Seine they would be unable to mount a coherent defence in northern Europe. Ironically, General Student's hastily constituted German 1st Parachute Army was to help resist Operation Market Garden.

As a result of their defeat in Normandy the Germans lost a quarter of a million troops and almost all their armour. Recovery from this seemed impossible and this situation lulled the Allies into a false sense of security.

The Red Ball Highway referred to routes used by the Red Ball Express. Following the Allied breakout from Normandy they needed to find a way of keeping almost thirty divisions resupplied. This was achieved by truck convoys that ran from 25 August to 16 November 1944.

A GMC 6x6 supply truck gets stuck in the mud. Keeping all the Allied armies supplied was a balancing act – availability of resources would have a direct impact on Operation Market Garden in mid-September 1944.

The Red Ball Express was run predominantly by African-American soldiers.

Ike in good cheer. After walking through the carnage of the Falaise Pocket, Allied Supreme Commander General Dwight Eisenhower seemed to concur that the German army was a spent force.

Field Marshal Montgomery managed to persuade Eisenhower that he should use Lieutenant General Miles Dempsey's British 2nd Army and the newly formed 1st Airborne Army to conduct a left hook through the Netherlands and into Germany.

Montgomery in conference with Lieutenant General Brian Horrocks (on the left). Although three corps were to be committed to Operation Garden, the ground element of the attack, the key role, fell to Horrocks's 30th Corps.

Horrocks had reservations about the whole enterprise. In order to reach Arnhem, his men would have to cross three canals and three major rivers. This photo and the following two were taken by members of Major General Robert Ross's 53rd (Welsh) Infantry Division, which formed part of 12th Corps. They were supplied by Gunner Alf Norman, who served with the 83rd Field Regiment, Royal Artillery.

The first water barrier was the Meuse-Escaut Canal, running through northern Belgium, which had to be bridged before the British 2nd Army could advance into the Netherlands. Horrocks secured De Groot bridge, a crossing to the west of Neerpelt, on 10 September 1944.

In case the Germans blew all the bridges in the path of 30th Corps, Montgomery and Horrocks gathered bridging equipment and engineers at Bourg-Léopold to the south of the Meuse.

To facilitate 30th Corps' crossing of the Dutch waterways, Bailey bridges were stockpiled ready to replace damaged civilian bridges. These two examples were used by General Patton's US 3rd Army to get across the Seine at Mantes, west of Paris, on 19 August 1943. This constituted the Allies' first bridgehead over the river.

American troops launching a Bailey bridge by hand. The problem faced by Horrocks was that any bridging would have to come up the same road on which his corps was advancing.

A column of vehicles including a captured German half-track belonging to Major General Allan Adair's Guards Armoured Division. His command, comprising the Coldstream, Grenadier, Irish and Welsh Guards, had the task of cutting their way to Arnhem.

On 16 September Horrocks briefed his officers, explaining their mission and that as they had been given priority with resources they could not expect too much help from 8th and 12th Corps.

Pushing 30th Corps up a single exposed road, Highway 69, seemed an impossible task in the face of determined German resistance.

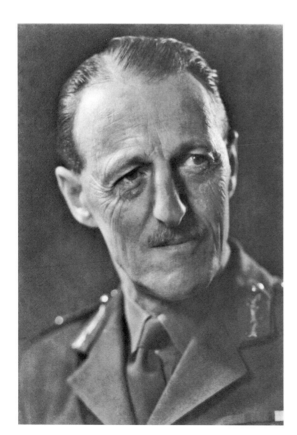

Major General Robert Knox Ross, commander of the 53rd (Welsh) Infantry Division. Lieutenant General Ritchie's 12th Corps only managed to secure a single narrow bridgehead over the Meuse-Escaut Canal prior to 17 September 1944. The advance of 12th Corps on Horrocks's left and 8th Corps on his right were to prove much too slow.

A much-graffitied Sherman. The Dutch hoped that the arrival of the Guards Armoured Division at Valkenswaard would herald liberation from Nazi occupation.

The ubiquitous Sherman M4 tank. The Guards' tanks would find themselves unprotected as they drove up Highway 69 with their flanks vulnerable to enemy fire.

The Guards' commander Major General Allan Adair travelled in a Cromwell command tank such as this one, which was photographed on 4 September 1944 during the liberation of Brussels. His division travelled 156km in just fourteen hours – such progress made Arnhem look achievable.

Another photo taken by the 53rd Infantry Division.

A squad of American GIs and supporting Sherman tank in Belgium in early September 1944. Note the Culin hedgerow-cutter on the front of the hull. US airborne forces were to play a key role in Montgomery's drive on Arnhem.

An Sd Kfz 251 being used as an ambulance by American and British medics in Chambois, August 1944. The half-track is in dunkel gelb with olivgrun sprayed on in irregular long thin streaks. The sign on the rear door indicates that the vehicle belonged to the 232nd Infantry Division. Such images helped persuade the Allies that the German armed forces were finished.

Maintaining supplies to General Patton's US 3rd Army meant that only General Horrocks's 30th Corps was adequately resourced to conduct Operation Garden.

African-American anti-aircraft gunners protecting a convoy with a 40mm Bofors gun. German flak would play havoc with the Allies' para drops and glider landings.

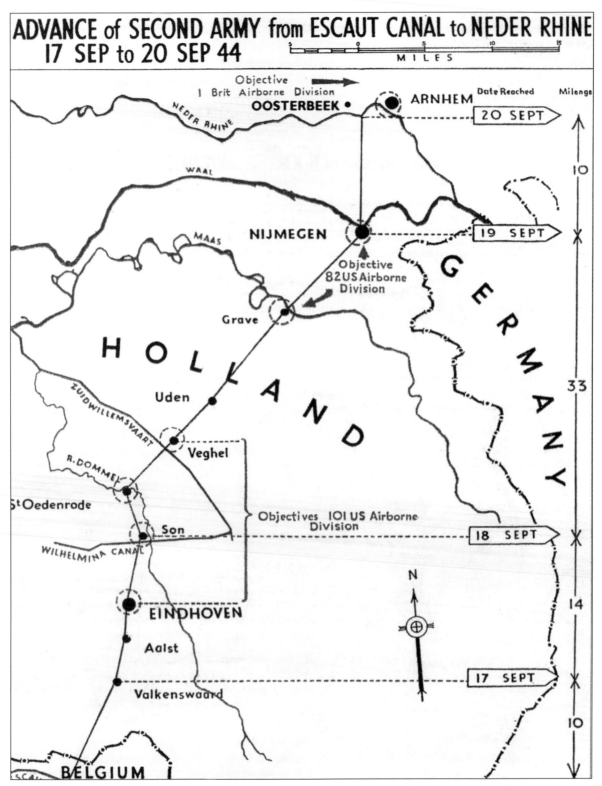

ADVANCE of SECOND ARMY from ESCAUT CANAL to NEDER RHINE
17 SEP to 20 SEP 44

MILES

Objective
1 Brit Airborne Division
OOSTERBEEK •   **ARNHEM**

Date Reached   Milenge

NEDER RHINE

20 SEPT

WAAL

10

NIJMEGEN

19 SEPT

MAAS

Objective
82 US Airborne
Division

G E R M A N Y

Grave

H O L L A N D

33

Uden

ZUIDWILLEMSVAART

Veghel

R. DOMMEL

St Oedenrode

Objectives 101 US Airborne
Division

18 SEPT

Son

WILHELMINA CANAL

N

14

EINDHOVEN

Aalst

17 SEPT

Valkenswaard

10

BELGIUM

Map showing the advance of Second Army and the objectives of the airborne divisions.

Chapter Two

An Airborne Market

Operation Market was to be carried out by the 1st Airborne Corps, commanded by a British officer, Lieutenant General Sir Frederick Browning – better known as 'Boy' Browning. His corps comprised the tough US 101st Airborne Division, tasked with capturing and holding the road north from Eindhoven to Grave; the US 82nd Airborne Division, who were to take the bridge at Grave over the Maas as well as the railway and road bridges over the Waal at Nijmegen; and lastly the British 1st Airborne Division, who were to seize the bridges at Arnhem and establish a bridgehead north of the Dutch Rhine known as the Neder Rijn.

Browning's corps formed part of General Lewis H. Brereton's 1st Allied Airborne Army. This included a second airborne corps headquarters, that of Major General Matthew B. Ridgway's US 18th Airborne Corps. Ridgway was the most experienced airborne commander and had hoped he would be appointed to command the operation. Browning, though, was dual-hatted: acting not only as a corps commander, but also as Brereton's deputy commander. The 1st Allied Airborne Army had only come into being in early August 1944. Since then it had planned eighteen operations, none of which had come to fruition.

For Operation Market in total 35,000 men with all their equipment, jeeps and guns were to be airlifted by transport aircraft and around 2,500 gliders from twenty-four airfields. The available number of transport aircraft and towing planes meant that these forces would be shifted in airlifts on successive days. While the two US divisions were proven veterans of Normandy, 1st Airborne had missed out – it was the British 6th Airborne Division that had fought there.

The British 1st Airborne Division, under the command of Major General Robert 'Roy' Urquhart, comprised the 1st and 4th Parachute Brigades, the 1st Airlanding Brigade (gliders) and the 1st Polish Parachute Brigade. General de Guingand was aware that Browning's airlift was inadequate and the operational implications of this:

Our transport aircraft resources were insufficient to drop the whole Corps in one day. The complete operation, which included reinforcement and resupply, would take four days in all. Another difficulty was that at Arnhem the country and enemy flak defences necessitated landing the 1st Airborne Division some eight miles from the town.

The Germans had placed anti-aircraft guns, not only to protect the bridges, but also the airfield at Deleen. The transport aircraft would have to fly near this if they attempted to deliver all the division actually around Arnhem. These problems sowed the seeds of 1st Airborne's destruction.

If, as planned, Horrocks could get to them within forty-eight hours, then the four-day airlift time frame was not a problem, because it would be simply reinforcing an established bridgehead that had linked up with the advancing ground forces. Should Horrocks be delayed then the airborne timetable looked like a recipe for disaster.

The airborne forces were not informed of the operation any sooner than 30th Corps. Lieutenant Colonel John Frost, commanding the 2nd Battalion of the Parachute Regiment, recalled:

On 15 September Brigadier Gerald Lathbury briefed his subordinate commanders of 1st Parachute Brigade. We were to take part in a great offensive which had the ultimate aim of surrounding the Ruhr and making it impossible for the Germans to continue the war.

Maps and aerial reconnaissance showed that at Arnhem there were three bridges running east to west, comprising a road bridge, a pontoon bridge and a railway bridge. Control of all three offered the opportunity to get ground forces across the river quickly. To the west of Arnhem were the towns of Oosterbeek, Wolfhezen and Heelsum. The designated drop and glider-landing zones were beyond these, not to the south of the river around Driel and Elden as might be expected.

Frost and his colleagues were not happy with the spread of the drop zones in the Arnhem area. For a start they were on the north side of the river and miles from the main Arnhem road bridge. This meant the element of surprise would be quickly lost and potentially hamper their ability to get to Arnhem. If the Germans responded swiftly to the threat then Frost would be in trouble from the start.

In light of the Allies' overwhelming air superiority, the presence of enemy flak seemed a spurious excuse for not dropping nearer Arnhem. Surely, reasoned Frost, as he listened to the briefing, fighter-bombers could easily neutralise the Germans' anti-aircraft guns beforehand? The air force planners also argued against a landing to the south of Arnhem, because the ground was not suitable for gliders or indeed paratroops. Frost was baffled when the assembled officers were informed that on

D-Day plus 2 the Polish Parachute Brigade, under Major General Stanislaw Sosabowski, would be dropped south of the main bridge!

There was more bad news: the air forces were only going to fly one sortie on the first day. The first lift would involve 157 parachute aircraft and 358 towed gliders. The single initial drop meant only half of 1st Airborne could be delivered, and half of those on the ground would have to defend the drop zones. The result was that a distance of some eight miles would separate the drop zones from the 1st, 2nd and 3rd Parachute Battalions, which were to secure northern Arnhem, the bridges and the western part of the town respectively.

In light of the need for a swift build-up at Arnhem, this was clearly a serious mistake. It also meant that German anti-aircraft gunners would be fully alert by D-Day plus 1. The planners were playing Russian roulette with the weather, which if it turned bad would delay the second airlift. This was to involve 124 parachute aircraft and 301 towed gliders, and the latter would be a very tempting target for enemy flak. The third airlift bringing in the Poles was much smaller, using 114 aircraft and just thirty-five gliders.

Frost appreciated that his primary objective was to seize the main bridge at Arnhem. The approaches to this were horribly exposed, because the road on either bank rose up elevated ramps above the surrounding buildings to reach the bridge. Intelligence showed that the pontoon bridge had been partially dismantled, though he still had to secure the railway bridge that was about two miles to the west of the town. While he was confident he could take the northern end of the main bridge, securing the south was another matter. Frost decided that his A Company would head for the main bridge while C Company would grab the railway bridge near Oosterbeek. The latter unit could then cross and link up with A Company at the southern end of the main bridge.

On the whole, Major General Urquhart was optimistic his division would succeed and be relieved in a timely manner:

> It was estimated that 30th Corps might reach the Zuider Zee, ninety-nine miles from the start line, between two and five days after crossing the Dutch-Belgian border. They were expected to link up with us in Arnhem between the second and fourth days – a distance of sixty-four miles.

Urquhart felt this was achievable in light of the British Army storming almost 300 miles between the end of August and 11 September. This had taken them from the Seine to the Escaut Canal. However, he did add a note of caution: 'Yet it needed no military genius to detect the snags'.

General Eisenhower with members of the US 101st Airborne Division on the eve of Operation Overlord. For Operation Market these Normandy veterans were tasked with seizing Eindhoven and the road north to Grave on the River Maas.

Like D-Day, Operation Market used a combination of paratroopers and glider-borne infantry to spearhead the assault. Cargo gliders were also used to bring in heavier support weapons.

The use of towed gliders greatly influenced the selection of landing zones, especially to the west of Oosterbeek.

A member of the 101st Airborne guarding prisoners in Normandy. This division, along with the US 82nd and the British 1st Airborne Divisions, formed the 1st Airborne Corps.

The principal transport aircraft were the Douglas C-47 Skytrain and C-53 Skytrooper, the latter being the specialised paratroop variant. Supplied to the RAF under Lend-Lease, the C-47 was dubbed the Dakota by the British.

Lieutenant General Lewis H. Brereton, commander of the Allied 1st Airborne Army. This only came into being in August 1944 as a way of grouping the Allies' airborne forces together. It had two corps headquarters, including Lieutenant General Sir Frederick Browning's 1st Airborne Corps.

Major General Matthew B. Ridgway (second from the left) in Sicily in 1943. He commanded Brereton's 18th US Airborne Corps and was by far the most experienced Allied airborne commander, but Browning was Brereton's deputy.

The British Airspeed AS.51 Horsa troop/cargo-carrying glider, capable of taking up to twenty-five men. It was first deployed operationally in Norway in 1942 and was used the following year during Operation Huskey and the invasion of Sicily. Its biggest claim to fame was its role in D-Day and subsequently Operation Market.

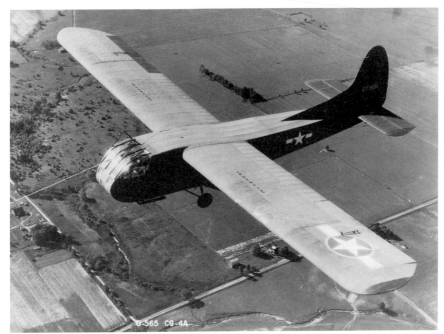

An American Waco CG-4A glider, which in British service was known as the Hadrian after the Roman emperor. This design also proved itself in Sicily and Normandy. Its capacity was smaller than the Horsa and it could only take thirteen soldiers.

Wacos gathered in England prior to the airlift to the Netherlands on 18 September 1944 in support of the US 101st Airborne Division.

Transport for the airborne forces was provided by the ubiquitous American jeep.

The jeep could be airlifted by both the Horsa and Waco gliders and equipped the reconnaissance squadron of the British 1st Airborne Division.

British 1st Airborne was also equipped with 6-pounder (57mm) anti-tank guns, seen here belonging to the Canadian Army, 75mm pack howitzers and 17-pounder anti-tank guns. The 6-pounder was transported with its jeep tow vehicle in a Horsa. Before loading the gun shield was removed.

The 1st Airborne Division's largest anti-tank weapon was the 17-pounder, which was transported in the Hamilcar heavy cargo glider.

The British had developed an air portable tank known as the Tetrarch, which saw limited service during D-Day. However, its thin armour and poor armament comprising a 2-pounder (40mm) gun meant it was not deployed in support of Operation Market.

The standard light support weapon for Britain's airborne forces was the Mk 3 Bren light machine gun, introduced in 1944. This was a shorter and lighter version of the Mk 1. The Bren gun was simple and above all reliable and accurate.

Lieutenant General Frederick Browning, commander of the 1st Airborne Corps, after a visit to Normandy. Browning was to remain unperturbed by the presence of the 2nd SS Panzer Corps in the Arnhem area.

Major General Stanislaw Sosabowski, commander of the Polish Parachute Brigade, with Browning. The Poles were supposed to reinforce 1st Airborne at Arnhem.

The cramped cockpit of the Horsa glider, which required two crew. This particular example is a reproduction built for the movie *A Bridge Too Far* and resides in the Cobbaton Combat Collection.

Chapter Three

What Panzers?

The German defence of the region selected for Operation Market Garden was in a very safe pair of hands. Field Marshal Walther Model had replaced von Kluge as commander-in-chief West and commander of Army Group B on 18 August 1944, just as the battle for Normandy was reaching its climax. The latter's predecessors had been Field Marshal von Rundstedt and Field Marshal Rommel, who had initially been responsible for the two respective commands. Model was used to firefighting on the Eastern Front and was not the sort of commander to panic when put under pressure. Nor was he going to buckle when faced with an unexpected situation such as a surprise airborne attack.

When Horrocks issued his orders for the drive to Arnhem they included the following intelligence appraisal of Model's available forces in the area:

Enemy
German Commander Model – very experienced, has fought a lot on Russian front. Troops opposing us mostly airborne formations under General Student [1st Parachute Army] – and in particular opposite Joe's Bridge [De Groot Bridge over the Escaut Canal], 6th Parachute Regiment, commanded by Van [von] der Heydte. Additional troops arriving from Germany every day, mostly consisting of young paratroopers, highly indoctrinated, therefore very brave, while their NCOs are the best and most experienced in the German Army.

This seemed to suggest that there would be some tough fighting ahead, but against lightly equipped German airborne forces that lacked heavy weapons. Student's 1st Parachute Army was a weak ad hoc formation of corps strength, thrown together in early September to block the Antwerp-Maastricht gap. Further to the west General von Zangen's 15th Army was largely bottled up around the Scheldt Estuary and the Channel ports.

Largely on the assumption that this was a spent force, Montgomery in early September failed to stop the escape of 15th Army. This had created a defensive pocket south of the Scheldt Estuary and west of Antwerp. It was then able to withdraw across the Scheldt to the islands of Walcheren and Beveland. From there it could send troops east to Breda and then Tilburg to the north-east of Eindhoven.

Lieutenant Colonel Frost, with 1st Airborne, was also led to believe that German defences were very weak:

> The German Army was thought to have taken such a beating in Normandy that all remaining availability was facing 30th Corps on the Albert canal and that there was nothing else in reserve.

General Horrocks's eyes, while weighing up his situation map, alighted on the Betuwe, the low-lying ground between Arnhem and Nijmegen, which was sandwiched between the Rhine and the Waal. This, for obvious reasons, was dubbed 'The Island', and it seemed to Horrocks that this would present the Germans with an ideal defensive buffer for preventing him from reaching Arnhem. Even once the crossings at Nijmegen were taken by the US airborne forces, if Model held on to the triangle formed by Oosterhout, Bemmel and Elst then he could still conduct a successful defence south of Arnhem. Intelligence indicated that apart from local administrative and police units, the Germans had nothing with which to defend the area.

However, just twenty-eight miles north-east of Arnhem was the newly arrived headquarters of General Willi Bittrich, commander of the 2nd SS Panzer Corps. This comprised the very battered remains of the 9th and 10th SS Panzer Divisions that had fought in Normandy under Walter Harzer and Heinz Harmel. Although these divisions had suffered heavy losses, they avoided being trapped in the Falaise pocket and retained some of their artillery, tanks and self-propelled guns. These were more than capable of taking on lightly armed airborne troops.

Writing in 1960, General Horrocks, in his memoirs *A Full Life*, claimed he had no knowledge of Bittrich's presence:

> Quite unknown to me, and as far as I can make out, also our intelligence service… the 9th and 10th SS Panzer Divisions arrived in the Zutphen area… They might have been sent almost anywhere else, but no! Fate… decreed that they should arrive just at this moment in an area from which they could intervene rapidly in the Arnhem battle.

Subsequently, in his *Corps Commander* book, Horrocks clarified this further and pointed the finger:

> I had no idea whatever that the 9th and 10th Panzer Divisions were refitting just north-east of Arnhem, nor had Dempsey so far as I know, yet both

Montgomery and Browning knew that they were there, as they had been identified by air photographs. I can only imagine that both were determined not to scrap once again the operation of the Airborne Army.

Like Model, General Bittrich was experienced in handling difficult situations and was more than capable of taking the initiative if his chain of command was slow or disrupted. Bittrich's presence meant that the Germans would have the ability to feed reinforcements into 'The Island' to obstruct Horrocks's advance. To make matters worse for Horrocks, to the west of his route the Germans could call on not only elements of Student's paratroops, but also the 59th Infantry Division, while to the east were the 15th and 41st divisions. The speed with which the Germans were to react was to come as a nasty shock to both Montgomery and Horrocks.

Further south, Horrocks was aware that he was opposed by German paratroops who were holding the crossing over the River Dommel, which led to the Dutch town of Valkenswaard. Horrocks soon learned that there were German tanks in the vicinity of Valkenswaard. Two scout cars from the Household Cavalry dashed up the road through enemy positions until the bridge was in sight. This patrol, led by Lieutenant Buchanan-Jardine, discovered that the bridge could take the weight of armour after they watched a German Panzer Mk IV cross. The scout cars then drove back to their lines under fire. The Germans took revenge for this incursion. After locating the café from where the British had viewed the bridge, they proceeded to execute three Dutch civilians.

To make matters worse for Montgomery, Browning and Horrocks, Model was to be alerted first hand by the paratroop drop at Arnhem. On 17 September 1944 he and his staff officers were lunching in a hotel at Oosterbeek, the small town just six miles to the west of Arnhem. After getting over the shock, Model immediately drove off to liaise with Bittrich. 'Not only did the Panzer Divisions have an overwhelming superiority in firepower, despite their recent losses,' noted Horrocks, but 'to make matters worse, they had trained in Normandy specially to combat airborne troops'. The location of Bittrich's tanks and his panzergrenadiers did not bode well for Urquhart's paratroops.

Alarm bells did begin to ring about the presence of these tanks at Arnhem. Major Brian Urquhart (no relation to British 1st Airborne Division commander Major General Urquhart) was Browning's intelligence chief and he did not believe the dismissive assessments of the German armed forces. His concerns had been sparked by intelligence supplied by the Dutch resistance via Dempsey's British 2nd Army headquarters. This warned of increasing German strength in the Market Garden area and mentioned 'battered panzer formations believed to be in Holland for refit'.

This report lacked confirmation and was not included in the summaries passed up to Montgomery and Eisenhower, the Allied Supreme commander. Major Urquhart, though, was convinced that there were elements of two panzer divisions in the Arnhem area. What was not clear was if they were just passing through or had stopped to refit.

Major Urquhart felt that Market Garden was flawed because, as he noted, it:

> depended on the unbelievable notion that once the bridges were captured, 30th Corps' tanks could drive up this abominably narrow corridor… and then walk into Germany like a bride into a church. I simply did not believe that the Germans were going to roll over and surrender.

Urquhart detected a determination by Browning to get their airborne forces into action before the end of the war, come what may. He felt that Browning's statement that the object of their mission was to 'lay a carpet of airborne troops down over which our ground forces can pass' trivialised what they were trying to achieve. Urquhart took it on himself to do all he could to substantiate the Dutch reports, and on 12 September requested a Spitfire photo reconnaissance flight over Arnhem. He knew that high-level photography might miss tanks lurking under trees, or camouflage netting, but the Spitfire was capable of taking low-level oblique pictures.

Shortly afterward Major Urquhart was furnished with five photos that confirmed his worst fears. 'There, in the photos,' recalled Urquhart 'I could clearly see tanks – if not on the very Arnhem landing and drop zones, then certainly close to them'. He immediately reported his findings to General Browning, who brushed them aside. Browning suggested that they were lame ducks and were not operational. This renewed naysaying was the final straw. Urquhart had made himself unpopular with the corps' other staff officers, who claimed he was suffering from nervous exhaustion, hence his anxiety over Market Garden. On medical grounds Urquhart was sent home.

Nonetheless, concern about the arrival of the 9th and 10th SS did reach much further up the chain of command. With Market Garden less than 48 hours away, Eisenhower's British intelligence chief, Major General Kenneth W. Strong, briefed Ike's chief of staff Lieutenant General Walter Bedell Smith. He explained that since early September the 9th and 10th SS divisions had vanished, but now the Dutch were reporting that they were in Holland near Arnhem. Smith rightly took the news to Eisenhower, as clearly the British 1st Airborne Division could not be expected to take on two enemy armoured divisions. Smith suggested that 1st Airborne be reinforced by a second division (Normandy veterans 6th Airborne were available).

This news placed Eisenhower in a difficult position: either he overrode Montgomery's plans and insisted on reinforcing 1st Airborne, or he cancelled Market Garden altogether. Neither was particularly attractive in light of the political difficulties it would cause. Nor was there the airlift capacity to get a second airborne division to Arnhem in a timely manner. Smith was sent to Brussels to discuss the problem with Montgomery. 'At least I tried to stop him,' said Smith, 'but I got nowhere. Montgomery simply waved my objections airily aside'. Montgomery reasoned that terrain and logistics would be his greatest obstacles, not German tanks. General Urquhart, commander of 1st Airborne, said all this was 'unknown to us'. Browning's instruction to Urquhart simply stated 'The latest intelligence will be sent to you up to the time of take-off'. This clearly did not happen.

While General Dempsey had tried to warn the paras, Montgomery and Browning did not. When 1st Airborne was briefed just prior to Market Garden they were not informed of the looming danger. Captain Alexander Morrison, officer commanding No.5 Flight Gilder Pilot Regiment, distinctly remembered that Brigadier Johnson made no mention of the threat:

> A tall, dapper-looking officer then moved to the centre of the platform and gave a brief summary of the known troops in northern Holland which, incidentally, made no reference to the two depleted divisions of German armour in the Arnhem area!

Captain Morrison's flight was tasked with flying in the 1st Airlanding Anti-Tank Battery under the command of Major Bill Arnold on 18 September, or D+1. Arnold's job was to support the 1st Parachute Brigade. His unit was equipped with 6-pounder (57mm) guns, which were not very good at dealing with enemy tanks at the best of times. However, his newly formed P Troop was armed with the much more powerful 17-pounders. Again Arnold had no inkling that his gunners would have to contend with elements of several panzer divisions. Major Haynes's 2nd Airlanding Anti-Tank Battery was to be airlifted in with Brigadier Hackett's 4th Parachute Brigade. Had they been forewarned they might have been better prepared.

The British airborne troops were also equipped with the new man-portable 83mm PIAT (Projector, Infantry, Anti-Tank) weapon. This had only entered service in 1943, when it first saw action during the Allied invasion of Sicily. It was effective out to about 100 metres when fired line of sight, or could manage three times this range when used for indirect fire. The projectile was technically capable of penetrating 100mm of armour. Although a simple design, it was far from perfect as it was difficult to cock (the firing mechanism was a large spring), had a powerful recoil and the projectile was often unreliable. Up to a quarter failed to detonate.

Fire support was provided by the American-built 75mm Pack Howitzer M1A1. This was designed so that it could be swiftly stripped down. The carriage trail could be split into pieces or removed whole. The trail sides featured large holes that helped to lighten the weight. Other airborne support weapons included the British Ordnance ML family of mortars (2, 3 and 4.2 inch). The weight of the 4.2 inch mortar was 116kg, with an effective range of 3,747 metres. These could be easily stripped down and packed into equipment containers for airborne operations. Explosives included the No.82 Grenade and the No.75 Hawkins Grenade. The latter was dual purpose and could be employed as a light mine. British airborne forces' small arms comprised the short-barrelled Mk 3 Bren light machine gun, the Mk 5 Sten submachine gun fitted with the wooden stock and the Lee Enfield rifle.

Field Marshal Walther Model was a highly competent commander. After Normandy the challenge he faced was putting together a credible defence in Belgium and the Netherlands. His 15th Army was trapped in the Scheldt estuary and the newly formed 1st Parachute Army was only an army in name.

Model being briefed by SS-Brigadeführer (Brigadier) Heinz Harmel, commander of the 10th SS Panzer Division *Frundsberg*. The presence of SS-Obergruppenführer (lieutenant general) Wilhelm 'Willi' Bittrich's weak 2nd SS Panzer Corps, comprising the 9th and 10th SS, in the Arnhem area, proved to be Model's greatest asset.

Harmel's 10th SS could muster at best 3,500 men and a few tanks. By 1944 Waffen-SS panzer divisions had an authorised strength of up to 15,000 troops and 6,000 support staff, with a panzer regiment and two panzergrenadier regiments plus supporting arms. It is therefore easy to see why Montgomery and Browning were so dismissive of the 2nd SS Panzer Corps.

SS-Obersturmbannführer (lieutenant colonel) Walter Harzer's 9th SS Panzer Division *Hohenstaufen* was much stronger than the *Frundsberg*, with about 6,000 men and some twenty tanks. This did not take into account its armoured cars and self-propelled guns. However, it was still far from a full division.

What was not clear to the Allies was whether the 2nd SS Panzer Corps was just passing through the Arnhem region or had stopped for a refit. The 9th SS was scheduled to return to Germany and had been ordered to hand its equipment over to its sister division.

Two self-propelled Panzer IV Möbelwagen anti-aircraft guns belonging to the 9th SS. Each was armed with a single 37mm flak gun, which was capable of engaging ground targets.

Although the 2nd SS Panzer Corps was weak in tanks, it had other fighting vehicles. In addition it was to be reinforced by a number of armoured units, including ten assault guns from the 280th Sturmgeschütz Brigade.

When Model began to muster reinforcements to thwart Operation Market Garden, these also comprised a company of fourteen Tiger Is. Two would be used against 1st Parachute Brigade at Arnhem and the rest supported counterattacks against 30th Corps' advance.

One weapon that was to be used to devastating effect against the Allies' airborne forces was the Nebelwerfer (fog-thrower) rocket launcher. This came in 150mm (six barrel) and 210mm (five barrel) calibre and was either mounted on a lightweight two-wheel split trail carriage or on a lightly armoured half-track. The Nebelwerfer was designed to deliver heavy short-range bombardments or smoke screens out to about 7,000 metres. The six barrels had to be fired separately to prevent the carriage from overturning and took just ten seconds. Reloading could be done in ninety seconds.

American troops being briefed on different types of grenade and mines. The large plate-like German Teller anti-tank mines on the left would prove a problem along Highway 69. The TM 43 was capable of penetrating the underneath of a Sherman tank. Photographic evidence shows that the Germans supplemented their demolition charges on Nijmegen bridge with mines and hand grenades.

Sherman crew taking on ammunition. Horrocks ordered 30th Corps to carry as much ammunition, fuel and food as they could, on the grounds that getting supplies up Highway 69 might prove difficult.

Chapter Four

Securing Eindhoven

Between 1300 and 1330 hours on 17 September 1944, some 6,769 men of the US 101st Airborne Division were dropped between Eindhoven and Veghel. Commanded by Major General Maxwell D. Taylor, these veterans of Normandy were known as the 'Screaming Eagles'. They were highly experienced in operating in bandit country where front lines did not exist. Self-sufficiency and initiative was a hallmark of their combat capabilities.

The operation proved an outstanding success, with the division suffering casualties of less than two per cent and the loss of five per cent of their equipment. The follow-up glider landings an hour later were not quite so successful. From a force of seventy gliders only fifty-three landed without harm.

Maxwell's job was to secure a series of bridges at Eindhoven, Son, St Oedenrode and Veghel, which crossed the Dommel River, Wilhelmina Canal, the Zuid Willems Canal and the Aa River respectively. The bulk of his division was delivered to the north-west of Son so that it could move south on Eindhoven and north on Veghel. Colonel Robert F. Sink's 506th Parachute Infantry Regiment was to reach Eindhoven in two hours. In addition Maxwell's 501st Parachute Infantry Regiment, under Colonel Howard R. Johnson, was dropped just to the south-west of Veghel. As well as taking the bridges Maxwell was expected to hold a fifteen-mile stretch of road, which was soon to be dubbed 'Hell's Highway'.

Colonel Sink's 506th Regiment encountered German resistance in Son and in the woods to the west. They then headed for the Wilhelmina Canal just south of Son and got to within fifty yards of the bridge before the Germans blew it up. It was now very apparent that a drop should also have been made south of the canal. Although Sink's engineers were able to build a footbridge from local lumber, it was midnight before his regiment was over. It was decided not to enter Eindhoven in the dark. In the meantime Maxwell's men were thwarted in capturing another bridge over the Wilhelmina Canal at Best to the west of Son.

Further north things went much more smoothly. At St Oedenrode the 101st took the crossing over the Dommel River. Likewise the 501st Regiment secured the Veghel bridges with little mishap. Nonetheless, in trying to hold open 'Hell's Highway'

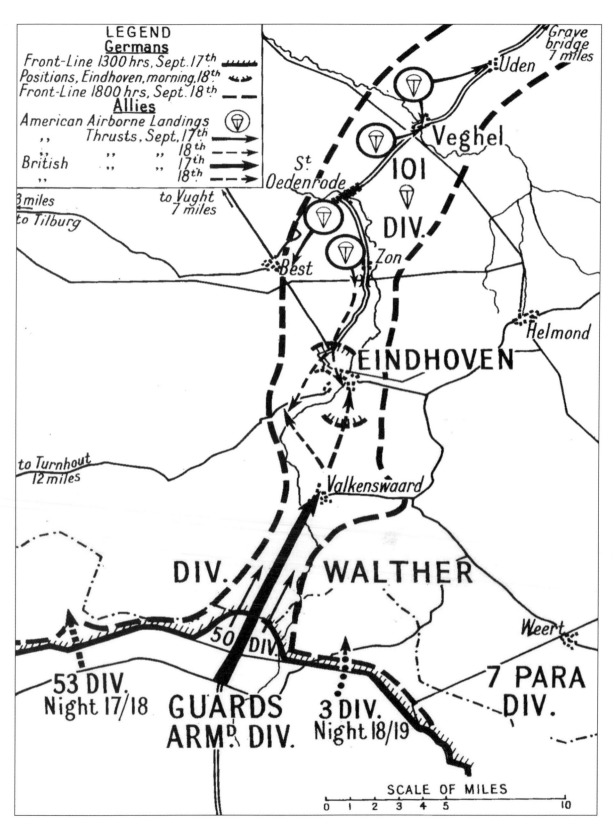

Market Garden: The Break-out, 17–18 September.

the 101st soon found themselves under fierce counterattack by German battle groups in the Veghel area.

Horrocks recalled:

As soon as the air armada came into view I ordered 'Zero hour 1435 Hours'. At 2pm precisely there was a sudden, deafening roar and a noise as though an express train were passing overhead. Our guns had opened their counter-artillery programme, and the battle of Arnhem was on. Under cover of the preliminary artillery bombardment the Irish Guards started moving into position just short of the start line.

Exactly on time Lieutenant Keith Heathcote's No.3 Squadron, 2nd Battalion Irish Guards (a tank regiment) revved up their engines and rolled forward. Some 350 guns laid down a rolling barrage 100 yards in front of Heathcote's crews. Beyond the falling shells RAF Typhoon fighter-bombers joined in delivering rockets onto the German positions. It seemed hard to believe that the dazed Germans could survive such a pounding – but they did.

Horrocks observed that 'From my command post the whole battlefield was visible and for the first ten minutes all seemed to be going well'. German gunners weathered the storm, however, and within the space of just two minutes accounted for nine of the Guards' leading tanks. Horrocks marvelled at the coolness of cousins Giles and Joe Vandeleur, colonels who commanded the 2nd and 3rd Battalions of the Irish Guards, which were tank and infantry units respectively. He noted they showed far less tension than if they had been Trooping the Colour on Horseguards in London.

The circling Typhoons delivered their rockets within 200 yards of the advancing infantry. Horrocks was delighted with the level of air cover he received. 'No Corps has ever had better air support than was provided for me that day,' he said with great satisfaction. By the evening the Guards' Armoured Division had got to the red-brick village of Valkenswaard.

On Horrocks's right, the plan was that Lieutenant General O'Connor's 8th Corps, consisting of the 3rd Infantry Division and the 11th Armoured Division, would attack between Neerpelt and Weert towards Helmond, which lay east of Eindhoven. On his left Lieutenant General Ritchie's 12th Corps, comprising the 15th and 53rd Infantry Divisions plus the 7th Armoured Division, would deploy as far as Turnhout, with the task of cutting its way to Tilburg to the west of Eindhoven then reaching the River Maas. In theory these attacks would greatly alleviate German pressure on the 101st Airborne at Eindhoven and ease the passage of 30th Corps northwards.

The reality was to prove somewhat different. Unfortunately neither O'Connor nor Ritchie was given explicit orders to press home their attacks with any great vigour. Both seem to have been under the impression that they were to do little more than 'lean on the enemy'. Horrocks did not help himself by telling Ritchie 'that he had grave doubts as to the possibility of his being able reasonably quickly to break out of his bridgehead...' This gave the distinct impression that the whole operation was going to be a slow slog rather than a desperate race against time.

In fairness, on 17 September Dempsey only had the resources to commit four of his nine divisions. A lack of transport meant that 8th and 12th Corps were unable to prepare adequately for Market Garden. The wait for bridging equipment meant that the 3rd Infantry Division was not to cross the Meuse-Escaut Canal until 19 September, when Horrocks should have been reaching Arnhem. While both corps were to suffer heavy casualties as the operation progressed, like 30th Corps they were clearly not imbued with a sufficient sense of urgency. There have since been dark mutterings that Eisenhower should have halted General Patton's US 3rd Army to the south. This could have freed up more supplies and transport for Montgomery, but such speculation is a largely nugatory exercise.

The following day, on the 18th, Colonel Sink's 506th Regiment moved out from its Wilhelmina Canal bridgehead and belatedly headed for Eindhoven. They bumped into a few German patrols and did not reach the city until midday. On the outskirts German resistance was encountered in the shape of a few 88mm self-propelled guns. Once in Eindhoven, Sink's men quickly rounded up the German garrison, which amounted to little more than a company of rear echelon troops. Not long after two British armoured cars from the Household Cavalry arrived from the north-west. However, the Sherman tanks of the Guards' Armoured Division did not appear for another five and a half hours. Market Garden was already twenty-four hours behind schedule. It was not a good start.

When the Guards finally crossed the Dommel at Eindhoven they edged their way through crowds of jubilant Dutch civilians. 'As the guardsmen rolled rapidly northwards,' said Horrocks '...they were greeted at the canal bridges and cross-roads by cheerful groups of tough-looking paratroopers from the 101st US Division, the men whose job it now was to protect our life-line to the rear'.

Horrocks added:

Their commanding General, Maxwell Taylor, told me that the initial landing had been completely successful, the best the Division had ever carried out, an entire regiment had come down in full view of their Commander.

The Americans, making use of the local Dutch telephone network, let the British know about the blown Wilhelmina Canal bridge at Son and the Guards' engineers were soon at work building a replacement.

To the north the Americans experienced a few light counterattacks around Veghel, but these had not yet caused any real problems. At Best, though, a battle soon developed over control of the other Wilhelmina bridge. Colonel John H. Michaelis sent his 2nd Battalion, 502nd Parachute Infantry Regiment, but they were countered by elements of the German 59th Infantry Division. Despite air support the lightly equipped paratroopers made little progress and the Germans blew the bridge.

The second airlift brought in welcome reinforcements and supplies for Maxwell's overstretched division. Some 440 gliders took to the air along with 121 bombers. The gliders delivered two battalions of Colonel Harper's US 327th Glider Infantry Regiment and other divisional units amounting to 2,579 men. This was at a cost of twenty-two gliders which did not arrive. The supply drop by the bombers was not successful, with only half the supplies being recovered. By now 30th Corps was on its way to link up with the 82nd Airborne Division. Phase one of Market Garden, despite the delays, had been successfully completed.

The Douglas C-47 Skytrain was a military version of the DC-3 airliner and had a strengthened floor and larger cargo-handling door on the port side. Over 10,000 had been produced by the end of the war, with 1,200 supplied to the RAF. In a supply role it could carry up to 2,700kg (6,000lb) of equipment. When used as a paratroop aircraft it was fitted with folding benches that could take twenty-eight fully armed troops.

The skies over the Netherlands were filled with billowing parachute canopies on 17 September 1944. Major General Maxwell Taylor's US 101st Airborne Division was dropped between Eindhoven and Vegel. It was a textbook drop, though the follow-up glider landings were not quite so successful.

Men of the 506th Parachute Infantry Regiment, US 101st Airborne, pick through the shattered wreckage of two Hadrian gliders that crashed into each other on the landing zone near Son. Two casualties are visible on the ground to the left and right. Inevitably the pilots were often fatalities in this type of collision.

A selection of British 'soft skinned' vehicles including jeeps. Horrocks's 30th Corps had some 20,000 vehicles that were going to have to drive up Highway 69 to link up with the airborne forces.

At 1400 on 17 September 1944 Horrocks's field artillery and self-propelled guns, such as the Sexton armed with a 25-pounder, and British fighter-bombers pounded German positions north of the Meuse-Escaut Canal.

The tanks of the 2nd Battalion, Irish Guards made good progress for the first ten minutes, but within twenty minutes the Germans had knocked out nine of the lead tanks. Each time this happened the road was blocked and the damaged tanks had to be shunted out of the way. This shot shows a Guards' Sherman Firefly, armed with a 17-pounder gun, negotiating two of the German anti-tank gunners' victims.

Two more burnt-out Guards' Shermans abandoned at the roadside. The narrow highway was only wide enough for one vehicle at a time – from the very start it was difficult to see how 30th Corps would be able to stick to its timetable.

British infantry plod past an abandoned 88mm flak gun. This, plus the German Pak 40 75mm and Teller mines, accounted for most of the Guards Armoured Division's initial losses.

Smiling Dutch girls welcome the crew of a Guards' Sherman by offering them apples.

On Horrocks's left the neighbouring 12th Corps advanced to support his flank. Late on 17/18 the 53rd (Welsh) Division attacked across the Meuse-Escaut Canal near Lommel. These carriers belonging to the 53rd are escorting captured German paratroops to the rear. The Bren gunner in the lead vehicle is clearly not taking any chances.

The British 17-pounder anti-tank gun was much heavier than its 6-pounder predecessor and had to be towed by the Morris Quad or M3 half-track. It was not very manoeuvrable on its own and had a habit of burying its split trail carriage when fired on soft ground. Compared to the Firefly the towed gun was not much help on 'Hell's Highway'.

Highway 69 was soon dubbed 'Hell's Highway' for good reason. This carrier was completely flipped by a Teller mine that smashed the vehicle's hull plate.

Members of the Welsh Guards transporting a wounded German soldier on their Cromwell tank. Like the American Sherman, the British-built Cromwell was inadequately armed and armoured.

Northward-bound. Another Guards' Cromwell is giving members of the US 101st Airborne a lift. Between Veghel, Uden and Nijmegen Highway 69 was soon to come under vigorous counterattack by German units moving into the area.

The Guards Armoured Division linked up with the US 82nd Airborne at Grave to the south-west of Nijmegen. Curious Dutch civilians gather round their British liberators. Such gatherings continually stalled Horrocks's progress.

Chapter Five

Fight for Nijmegen

Montgomery, Dempsey and Horrocks had clearly decided to ignore the fact that the further north they went the harder things would become. Taking Eindhoven was the easiest bit. The geography and the Germans would increasingly conspire to derail things. Stage two at Nijmegen would rapidly develop into a major headache for all concerned.

Brigadier General Jim Gavin's 'All American' 82nd Airborne Division had a task that was far more complicated than the 101st's. Gavin's division would have to fight to secure and hold the bridges in the Nijmegen area, starting at Grave over the Maas River, then at Hatert over the Maas-Waal Canal and over the Waal River at Nijmegen. To confound matters, to the south-east of Nijmegen lay a large wooded plateau area that extended to the town of Groesbeek, beyond which lay the Reichswald forest. The rumour was that panzers were lurking there.

Gavin's men had to take the Groesbeek Heights, which overlooked the Waal and, so they thought, the rail and road bridges at Nijmegen. Securing this high ground was vital in order to protect Horrocks's right flank from counterattack when he arrived. The problem with this requirement was that the heights would soak up two-thirds of Gavin's division and force him to defend a perimeter of twenty-five miles with three lightly armed regiments. This would leave Gavin's men exposed from the very start.

In reality, the highway bridge at Nijmegen cannot be seen from the heights because they sweep south-westwards. If this had been realised at the time Gavin could have secured a perimeter just three miles from Nijmegen city centre and this would still have stopped the Germans from observing the bridges.

Instead Gavin designated three drop zones for his regiments, with the 504th to the south-west just north of the Maas and the village of Overasselt, the 505th to the south-east just below Groesbeek and the 508th dropping to the north-east of Groesbeek. The 504th's job would be to secure the crossing near Grave, which was west of its drop zone, while the others would take Groesbeek village and Groesbeek Heights respectively. Late in the day Gavin also instructed the 508th to send one of its battalions to Nijmegen as soon as possible. Ironically, although Gavin

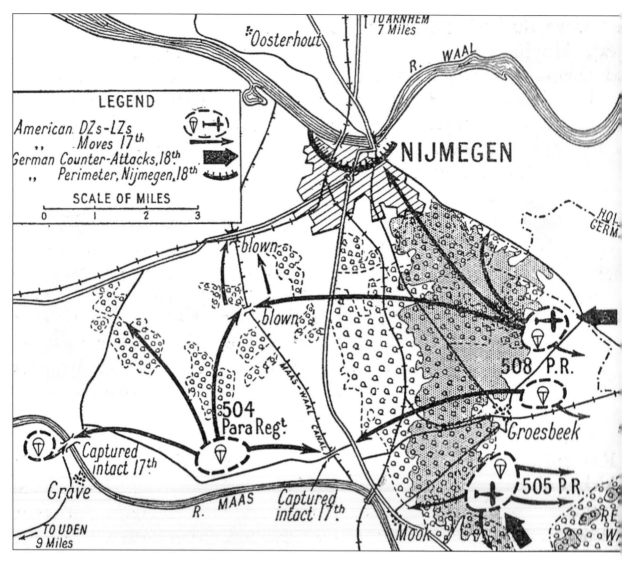

The Nijmegen 'Air-Head', 17–18 September.

had criticised the British for selecting drop zones eight miles from Arnhem, he found his division was dropping eight miles from Nijmegen and in thickly wooded country.

'The drop,' said Gavin 'was better than ever had been experienced'. Colonel Reuben H. Tucker's 504th jumped at 1313, supported by a subsidiary drop south of the Maas to the west of Grave. Caught from both directions the Germans failed to blow the bridge and by nightfall Grave itself had been secured. To the east another bridge was seized at Heumen, which crosses the Maas-Waal Canal. By the end of the day the 505th had successfully linked up with the 504th.

Now it was just a matter of taking Nijmegen. Colonel Roy E. Lindquist's 508th was the most stretched, as his men had to secure the high ground from Nijmegen, through Berg-en-Dal, to the south-east and on down to Wyler. They also had to move on Groesbeek in order to link with the 505th. To Gavin's relief, despite Dutch reports, no panzers came rumbling from the Reichswald, which meant that for the time being at least his eastern flank was safe. Lindquist's 1st Battalion did not set out for Nijmegen until seven hours after the landing. They then got lost in the side streets and ran into determined German resistance, which denied them the all-important road bridge.

On 17 September, in a quirk of fate, Field Marshal Model was just sitting down to lunch at the Tafelberg hotel in Oosterbeek. His staff officers, alarmed by the sound of aircraft and assuming they were bombers, ran to the windows. Instead they saw the paratroops of the British 1st Airborne Division filling the sky just two miles away. Their closeness inevitably fired Model into swift action. Summoning his staff car he then sped out of the hotel only to drop his bag. Officers frantically gathered up his papers and they drove away.

Initially Model may have thought the paras had come to kill or kidnap him. Once he got over the shock, he soon deduced that the Allies were probably trying to grab all the bridges north prior to crossing at Arnhem. If Model had been captured there is every possibility that the battle might have gone differently. Instead his car drove him twenty-eight miles north-east of Arnhem to Zutphen to consult with General Bittrich.

Once at Zutphen the pair examined their maps and took a critical tactical decision that would determine the outcome of the battle. Bittrich recalled:

In spite of the obscure situation at Arnhem and the likelihood of continued and increasing strong air landings in the area north of the Rhine, I advisedly chose to direct the main effort against the enemy forces in the Nijmegen area. So the 9th SS Panzer Division was ordered to prevent the British from seizing the Arnhem bridge and then push the Airborne Division out of the town to the west while additional forces were collected to seal them off from the north and west. The 10th SS Panzer Division was dispatched to the south to prevent the British Second Army from occupying the all-important bridges over the River Waal at Nijmegen.

Thanks to the presence of the 2nd SS Panzer Corps, Model had just about sufficient forces to counter Market Garden. Crucially, Bittrich had immediately identified both of Horrocks's key objectives. If he had chosen to deal solely with 1st Airborne at first, that would have weakened the German defences at Nijmegen with predictable results. Likewise, if he had concentrated on the latter first it would have allowed 1st Airborne to consolidate its hold on Arnhem.

By dividing his command, Bittrich moved to thwart the Allies at two locations at the same time, while reinforcements were also summoned to attack Horrocks from the east and the west. The battle now hung on how quickly 30th Corps could fight its way north. Just before the British took Arnhem bridge, the reconnaissance unit of the 9th SS rolled south and onto Nijmegen to oppose Colonel Lindquist's men.

General Browning, whose headquarters was not far from Gavin's command post, had arrived on the 17th in a fleet of thirty-six gliders. These would have been much better deployed airlifting an extra infantry battalion to Nijmegen or Arnhem. There was not much Browning could do to help, especially as the 101st was under the command of 30th Corps. He had established contact with the 82nd but no one else. Worryingly, the latter had received a message from the Dutch resistance via the telephone network, which ominously stated 'Germans winning over the British at Arnhem.'

By a stroke of bad luck the entire plans for Operation Market were allegedly discovered in a crashed Waco glider and rushed to General Student's headquarters at Vught. Fortunately for the Allies, his 1st Parachute Army was cut in two by the airborne invasion and his communications were down. Student was unable to contact Model for almost ten hours. The captured plans were eventually radioed to Model at Terborg, but because they were so detailed Model refused to believe that they were real. If, reasoned Model, Arnhem bridge was the goal, why had the British landed eight miles to the west? He anticipated another attack further to the north-east. As a result Model did not inform Bittrich. It has been suggested that these plans came from one of Browning's gliders.

Once Gavin's second airlift had taken place, Browning asked him to secure Nijmegen's two bridges. This was urgent because 30th Corps was scheduled to arrive at 1800 on 18 September. They did not know that Horrocks was not yet in Eindhoven. Gavin decided to throw the 505th into a frontal attack, while the 504th struck from the flank. Meanwhile his own flanks were coming under increasing pressure from the Germans, who were slowly feeding reinforcements into the area.

When the Guards eventually arrived, they began to push toward the Waal with the assistance of the 82nd. It soon became apparent that the Germans were well entrenched in Hunner Park and around Valkhof, covering the southern approaches to the road bridge. To the west, on 20 September, the 504th dramatically paddled across the Waal in open boats to seize and hold open the northern end of the Nijmegen bridges for Horrocks's Grenadier and Irish Guards.

The crossing by Major Julian Cook's 3rd Battalion, 504th, was covered by RAF Typhoons and gun fire from thirty Shermans belonging to the Irish Guards. Their flimsy assault boats offered no protection from the devastating fire laid down by the Germans on the far bank. Just half the craft made it, but the gallant survivors then swung east to assault the Germans in the Hof van Holland area that screened the railway. They also attacked Lent, through which both the railway and the road headed north, which finally cracked the German defences.

The American paratroopers climbed onto the road bridge just as four tanks from the Guards' Armoured Division arrived at the southern end. Brigadier Harmel ordered the SS to blow the bridge, but this did not happen. In the meantime, two German anti-tank guns claimed two of the approaching tanks, but they were then crushed by the others which linked up with the 504th. By 1910 the crossings of the Waal were in Allied hands.

Brigadier General Jim Gavin, commander of the US 82nd Airborne Division, was a veteran of the drops on Sicily and in Normandy. He served as the 82nd's assistant divisional commander on D-Day and assumed full command on 8 August 1944. His mission at Nijmegen was complicated by the need to capture the heights to the south-east.

The imposing Nijmegen road bridge over the River Waal was Gavin's primary objective. His other widespread objectives would prove a distraction.

Members of the US 82nd Airborne being briefed just before Operation Market. They had a total of four key bridges to secure over the Maas, Maas-Waal Canal and the Waal.

US paratroopers heading for their drop zone. The 82nd Airborne's three Parachute Infantry Regiments employed three drop zones, which required them to defend a twenty-five mile perimeter south of Nijmegen.

Men of the 504th Parachute Infantry Regiment engaging the enemy. Their first job was to secure the crossings at Grave and Hartert. They then had to force a crossing over the Waal.

A Waffen-SS soldier lies where he fell on the Nijmegen road bridge. The wire on the left is either telephone cable or detonator cord leading to the demolition charges the Germans rigged up on the bridge. The southern approaches were well defended by the Germans, who were entrenched in Hunner Park and around the Valkhof. It required a three-pronged attack by the Grenadier Guards and the US 505th Parachute Regiment to clear the defenders.

In the meantime, it was decided to try and turn the Germans' flank by conducting a river crossing to the west of Nijmegen railway bridge. This was covered by around a hundred guns and self-propelled guns such as the Guards' Sextons, two squadrons of Irish Guards tanks and Typhoon fighter-bombers.

The men of the US 504th Regiment were issued with about thirty paddle-powered canvas craft. This was sufficient for two assault companies minus their heavy support weapons. They were met by German rifle and machine-gun fire as well as mortars, but still managed to force a crossing.

By 1700 on 20 September 1944 the 504th was closing in on the northern end of the railway bridge and the local German defenders tried to flee north across it and were cut down. Just as the light began to fail Sergeant Peter Robinson led four Grenadier tanks across the road bridge. Although two tanks were lost, the others smashed the German road block at the end.

A column of Shermans, led by a Sherman Firefly, rumbles across the Nijmegen road bridge. By 1910 hours on 20 September 1944 the crossing over the Waal was firmly in Allied hands.

British sappers clearing mixed explosives from the Nijmegen road bridge. These included boxes of grenades and various types of mines. Although the Germans had rigged the bridge for demolition they failed to bring it down.

US airborne troops watch Guards' Cromwell tanks stream northwards over the Waal.

Divisional self-propelled guns in the shape of Sextons experience a hold-up while crossing the road bridge. The dead German soldier photographed earlier is just visible on the pavement to the right of the guard box.

This photo was taken at the end of September 1944 and shows the level of damage the street-fighting in Nijmegen caused. To clear the Germans from the southern approaches of the road bridge required the destruction of many of the surrounding buildings.

German frogmen managed to blow up the central span of the Nijmegen railway bridge towards the end of the month. It was replaced by a DUKW ferry service until it could be repaired.

Chapter Six

Trapped at Arnhem

At 1240 hours on 17 September 1944 the pathfinders of the British 21st Independent Parachute Company dropped west of Oosterbeek. Their task was to prepare for the arrival of the 1st Airborne Division's gliders just twenty minutes later. It took fifty minutes for them to complete the landing and inevitably there were accidents as gliders hit trees, each other or nosedived.

At 1400 it was the turn of the paratroops and it was an hour and a half before everyone was ready. Brigadier Lathbury's 1st Parachute Brigade was to use three parallel routes into Arnhem. To the south Frost's 2nd Battalion would secure the railway bridge, the pontoon bridge and then the main highway bridge. The 1st Battalion was to take the high ground to the north of the city, while 3rd Battalion would take the Utrecht-Arnhem road to link up with Frost.

Major General Urquhart and his 1st Airborne had no way of knowing what would happen when they dropped to the west of Arnhem. General Browning had told them they were unlikely to be faced by more than a German brigade and a few tanks. In his book on the battle Urquhart reported:

> In and around Arnhem and Oosterbeek that day were some 6,000 German troops of mixed quality, ranging from the battle-hardened SS Grenadiers of the 9th and 10th Panzer Divisions and the 425 corporals of the SS school to those 'ear and stomach' battalions whose existence led some Allied intelligence staffs into loose thinking.

As already discussed, Urquhart knew nothing of the presence of the 9th and 10th SS at the time. In addition, intelligence officer Major Brian Urquhart was certainly not guilty of 'loose thinking'. Ten days before Operation Market 1st Airborne's intelligence summary assessed that the Germans could muster around three regiments of infantry drawn from a number of infantry divisions and possibly fifty tanks from the remains of a panzer division from Rotterdam to the German frontier. The tanks were believed to be somewhere north of Arnhem.

On 13 September, before Major Urquhart saw General Browning, the

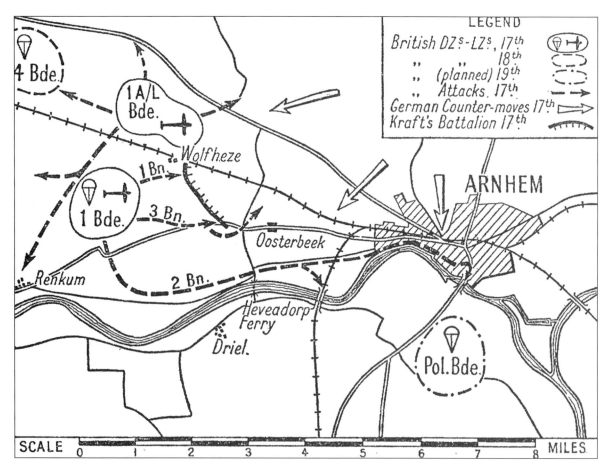

The Arnhem Landing, 17 September.

intelligence assessment stated that total German armoured strength in the region was 'probably not more than 50–100 tanks.' It also added 'There is every sign of the enemy strengthening the river and canal lines through Nijmegen and Arnhem, especially flak, but the troops manning them are not numerous and many are of low category.' The implication of this was that Horrocks's 30th Corps would have no trouble breaking through and that 1st Airborne had nothing to worry about.

Nonetheless, Major General Urquhart had decided to give his division some punch from the moment it landed. The first airlift brought in his headquarters, 1st Parachute Brigade, most of the 1st Airlanding Brigade and most of the divisional support units, including two of the three batteries of 75mm artillery. The 4th Parachute Brigade would be delivered the next day.

In light of the distance of the drop and landing zones from Arnhem, Urquhart decided the jeeps of Major Freddie Gough's 1st Airborne Reconnaissance Squadron should make a dash for the bridges. They would be followed by 1st Brigade, while the Airlanding Brigade held the landing zones. The plan then was that with the arrival of 4th Brigade and the Polish Brigade the division would form a strong defensive perimeter all around Arnhem, thereby creating a bridgehead for 30th Corps.

After the landings the paras first had to secure Wolfheze and Oosterbeek, which stood between them and Arnhem. It was not long before resistance was encountered at both locations and on the railway line into Arnhem. Gough's jeeps were held up and a problem was discovered with the range of the radios. When Frost's C Company reached the railway bridge the Germans demolished it. In the meantime the other two battalions were experiencing tough opposition from the Germans.

The faulty radios immediately impacted on Urquhart's control of the battle, because he found it difficult to communicate with his brigade commanders and Browning at Airborne Corps headquarters. Locating Lathbury, he discovered that the brigadier was having the same problem. Meanwhile, Frost's men observed that the central section of the pontoon bridge was missing, meaning that two of the three bridges were already out of action. Arriving at the main road bridge, which they found unguarded, they quickly occupied the buildings overlooking the northern ramp. Frost himself then arrived with his headquarters, followed by brigade headquarters (minus Lathbury) and Gough with a few of his jeeps.

Although Frost now held the northern end of the bridge, the Germans still controlled the southern end. During the night his A Company tried twice to force a crossing, but each time were driven back by machine-gun fire from a pillbox and an armoured car. Although the pillbox was silenced, the Germans attacked Frost's eastern flank and to add to the confusion tried to cross the bridge from the south.

In the morning a head count showed Frost had 500 men plus four 6-pounder anti-tank guns. He also had the support of the 75mm howitzers deployed near the church at Oosterbeek. This was adequate to defend his positions until the division sent reinforcements, and 30th Corps was expected by lunchtime on Tuesday 19 September. He also had around 100 German prisoners, most of whom belonged to the SS.

It did not take long for fighting to commence around Frost's positions on the morning of the 18th. In the confusion German lorries appeared outside Frost's HQ and were promptly shot up. The heat from still-burning German vehicles prevented his engineers from checking the bridge for demolition charges.

Then at 0930 the 9th SS reconnaissance unit returning from Nijmegen tried to cross back over the bridge it had safely traversed under twenty-four hours earlier. The first four vehicles sped by before anyone realised, but seven were caught by the paras using grenades, PIAT hand-held anti-tank weapons and a 6-pounder gun. There was carnage and smouldering wreckage was left scattered all along the northern ramp.

At the same time, German infantry with armoured cars and self-propelled guns renewed the attacks on Frost's perimeter, which encompassed about thirty buildings. While these could withstand small arms and mortar fire, when a 150mm self-propelled gun appeared it began to smash them to pieces. However, the paras managed to silence it.

Although Frost had gathered A and B companies, his C Company was missing and 1st Battalion was stuck on the outskirts of the city. Equally discouraging was the news that some of the prisoners came from the 9th SS Panzer Division. What Frost did not know was that both 1st and 3rd battalions had been badly mauled trying to get past the German positions at Den Brink, a wooded area to the north. Both had become bogged down around the St Elizabeth Hospital to the west. Lathbury had been wounded and Urquhart, with three others, was trapped in a house thanks to the presence of a German self-propelled gun parked just outside.

What the paras needed was reinforcing by the second airlift, which would bring 4th Parachute Brigade under Brigadier Shan Hackett. This would in turn release 1st Airlanding Brigade from its defensive role on the landing grounds. Two sorties should have been flown on the first day, which would have freed the Airlanding Brigade to help Lathbury. As it was 1st Airborne Brigade on its own had proved too weak to fully secure Arnhem on the 17th.

The Germans, expecting more airborne troops on the morning of 18 September, sent thirty Messerschmitts to attack the glider landing zones. Another ninety attempted to intercept the transport aircraft, but failed to get through their fighter escorts. At 1500 hours the 4th Parachute drop commenced, but it would be another four hours before they started toward Arnhem.

Advancing down the railway toward Oosterbeek, the newly arrived 156th Parachute Battalion found the road into town blocked by German troops. This was actually the forward defence line of the 9th SS, though Hackett was unaware of this. In the meantime, due to the absence of Lathbury and Urquhart, the commander of the Airlanding Brigade, Brigadier Pip Hicks, had assumed command of the division. Hackett was not happy about this, because although Hicks was older he was a junior brigadier. Hackett did not like being told how to deploy his command. Thanks to the disappearance of Urquhart, and perhaps more crucially the inadequate radios, 1st Airborne lacked a firm sense of direction and urgency.

All through 19 September the Germans probed Frost's perimeter using armoured cars, self-propelled guns and tanks supported by infantry. This led to bitter street-fighting as the Germans slowly drove the paras from their strongpoints established in the neighbouring buildings. Frost's casualties began to mount and water became an issue. An offer of surrender was made to him, but he simply ignored it. What he could not ignore was the failure of reinforcements to reach him. This was troubling, as it indicated that everyone else was experiencing difficulties. He had done all he could, but time was running out. In addition he knew that if the Polish Brigade dropped south of the bridge they would land in a hornets' nest.

Having failed to cut their way through to Frost, the survivors from the other battalions withdrew to take up positions to the east of Oosterbeek Church. Hackett and Hick's brigades were likewise frustrated in their efforts. The only good news was that Urquhart, after borrowing a jeep, managed to reach the divisional headquarters located in the Hartenstein Hotel at Oosterbeek. The glider landing by the Polish Parachute Brigade and the supporting resupply drop was a disaster. The drop for the three Polish parachute battalions was then postponed.

On the morning of 20 September a wounded Frost and the other survivors at Arnhem bridge were finally overwhelmed and captured. 'The SS men were very polite and complimentary about the battle we had fought,' said Frost 'but the bitterness I felt was unassuaged'. They had held the bridge for three days and three nights against heavily equipped elements of two SS panzer divisions. The battle for Urquhart's Oosterbeek perimeter now loomed.

The British 1st Airborne Division had three glider landing zones around Wolfheze to the west of Oosterbeek. This is Landing Zone Z near Wolfheze Woods and contains Horsa gliders and three of the larger Hamilcars. Most pilots successfully landed in the open fields, but some overshot and ended up among the trees. In this aerial view at least five have come to grief.

These men are at the Wolfheze crossroads. The para in the distance is equipped with a Bren gun, while the man in the foreground to the left is armed with the crude-looking PIAT anti-tank weapon. They are wearing the camouflage Denison 'para' smock, which was introduced in 1941 and could be worn over or instead of the battledress blouse. Equipment was always worn over it. Another sleeveless smock was worn over the equipment for the jump and removed after landing. Trousers are the standard battledress. Their heads are protected by the airborne rimless steel helmet.

The PIAT bomb could be fired to a range of just over 300 metres and could penetrate 100mm of armour. However, it was neither very accurate, nor very reliable.

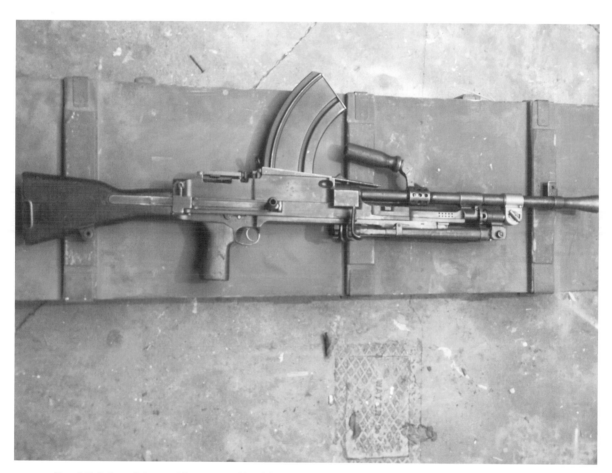

Para Mk 3 Bren light machine gun and its shipment box. This weapon was very popular and had good stopping power.

Men of Frost's 1st Battalion sheltering in a bomb crater near Wolfheze before commencing their dramatic assault on the bridges of Arnhem.

Anti-tank gunners of the 1st Airlanding Brigade with their 6-pounder, passing through Oosterbeek heading for Arnhem. Frustratingly this brigade could not assist the 1st Parachute Brigade because it initially had to protect the division's landing zones.

A 1st Airborne 6-pounder going into action. This weapon, used at close range, proved instrumental in helping to keep German armour at bay.

Lieutenant Colonel Frost was alarmed to discover that German prisoners taken in Arhnem were members of the 9th SS Panzer Division *Hohenstaufen*. This was the first inkling he had that he would be facing tanks.

An RAF reconnaissance photo showing the northern end of Arnhem road bridge – the key to Operation Market Garden. Most of the visible buildings formed part of Lieutenant Colonel John Frost's defensive perimeter, created by his 1st Battalion, 1st Parachute Brigade. This photo was taken the day after the landings as it shows the wreckage left by the ambushed 9th SS Panzer Reconnaissance unit.

Trouble in store. The SS at Arnhem were swiftly reinforced. The arrival of the ten assault guns from the 280th Sturmgeschütz Brigade plus other panzers soon pitted overwhelming firepower against the lightly equipped paras.

This Sturmhaubitze 42, armed with a 105mm howitzer, was able to blast Arnhem's buildings to smithereens. Such weapons slowly eroded Frost's defences around the bridge.

A StuG III photographed in the streets of Arnhem on 19 September 1944. Initially coordination with the 9th SS panzergrenadiers was not good, and this helped Frost's men to hold out for longer.

Frost's 1st Battalion managed to cling to their positions at the northern end of Arnhem bridge until 20 September 1944. In the face of German assault guns and other armoured fighting vehicles there was little more they could do.

Tough-looking members of the 9th SS picking through the debris after Frost's battalion was overwhelmed. The man on the right is carrying the Panzerfaust anti-tank weapon. It was not long before the Germans were attacking along the Utrechtseweg towards General Urquhart's positions at Oosterbeek.

Rather symbolically this German assault gun is parked near a British parachute in Arnhem. Montgomery and Browning seriously underestimated the very rapid response of the Germans.

Chapter Seven

Stalled in the Betuwe

By 21 September 1944 Horrocks was over the Waal, but his Guards Armoured Division only managed to fight its way two miles northward. The weather and German flak continued to deter the RAF, and Horrocks was annoyed that he was getting little air-to-ground support. This, and German control of Arnhem bridge, meant that the enemy was able to feed a steady flow of reinforcements into the Betuwe or 'The Island': the land between the Waal and the Neder Rijn.

Model and Bittrich had anchored their defence on Elst, which lay in the middle of 'The Island'. They also had forward defences at Oosterhout to the south-west and Bemmel to the south-east of Elst. Horrocks observed:

> I had realised, of course that 'The Island' with its dykes, high embankments carrying the roads, and deep ditches on either side was most unsuitable for armoured warfare.

In other words, it was a defenders' paradise. Elst in particular dominated the network of roads in the Betuwe and the railway line running from Nijmegen to Arnhem.

Horrocks hoped that Major General Thomas's 43rd Infantry Division might help break the log jam, but this first had to struggle up the congested road corridor that was under constant German attack. The US 101st Airborne managed to beat off a German counterattack at Son, but on 20 September the Germans had got into the village of St Oedenrode, halting all traffic. The 43rd Infantry experienced great difficulty in moving through both Eindhoven and Grave. Horrocks's traffic controllers could make little difference on the route in the face of the constant interference by the Germans.

It was hoped that the arrival of Major General Sosabowski's Polish Parachute Brigade, which had dropped near Driel south of the Neder Rijn, would turn the German flank. There remained, however, the vexed question of how they would get over the river with the Germans holding Arnhem bridge. Horrocks's plan was that the 43rd Infantry would hook left, cut their way to the Poles and then move on to

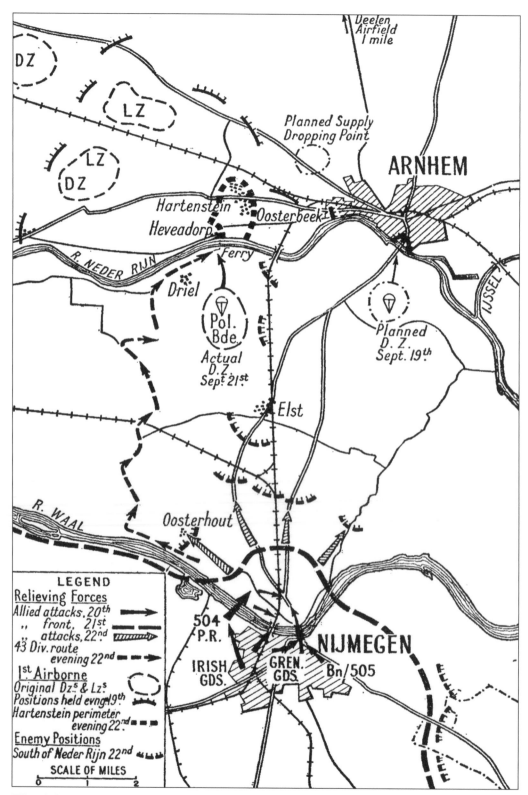

The Advance to the Neder Rijn, 20–25 September.

the beleaguered 1st Airborne Division. This operation was hampered by a growing shortage of artillery ammunition. On 22 September, under the cover of early morning fog, units of the Household Cavalry slipped past the Germans to reach Driel. This had been at a cost, because the fog lifted to reveal the tail end of the British column and a panzer knocked out three armoured cars.

Brigadier Essame, in command of the 214th Infantry Brigade from the 43rd Division, was tasked with cutting his way to Arnhem bridge some seven miles distant. Chaos ensued when part of his brigade was sent over the road bridge instead of the railway bridge at Nijmegen and he had to round up his scattered forces. Turning west at Oosterhout, Essame bumped into a battalion of German infantry supported by tanks and self-propelled guns. Because of the exposed landscape his 7th Somerset Light Infantry launched their attack without tank support. This failed, with the loss of Major Sidney Young.

It was only on the third attempt, with artillery support, that Essame managed to get through the determined German defences. Among the ruins of the village the Somersets rounded up 130 SS prisoners and captured a self-propelled gun and three tanks, one of which was undamaged. The British relief column consisted of tanks with infantry riding on them, followed by motorised infantry. Setting off just before dark, within thirty minutes they had covered the ten miles to Driel and the Poles. However, this success was marred by the Germans, who managed to get five Tiger tanks from Elst in between the two halves of the column.

Seeing the danger, Company Sergeant Major Philip, travelling in a carrier at the rear of the tank column, rammed the lead panzer and killed its commander. Then two platoons of infantry with PIAT hand-held anti-tank weapons and anti-tank mines were sent to 'clear up the mess'. In the dark these tank hunter teams bravely stalked their lumbering enemy. Three of the Tigers were knocked out, while the other two were abandoned by their crews, which indicated they were inexperienced.

The following day Horrocks learned that the survivors of Urquhart's division had abandoned Arnhem and were now trapped at Oosterbeek. This meant that taking Arnhem bridge would be even harder. He was also informed that 'Hell's Highway' had once more been cut. The route was being attacked from both sides, as well as shelled and mortared on a regular basis. While the stretched US 82nd and 101st Airborne Divisions were doing all they could, it was hardly fair to expect them to be able to perform like regular infantry divisions and protect the corridor when they lacked heavy equipment. Frustratingly, the slow advance of the British 8th and 12th corps did little to alleviate the pressure on Horrocks's lines of communication and his flanks.

All this was an unwanted distraction from the fighting in 'The Island'. Horrocks had little choice but to turn the 32nd Guards Brigade south, while the US 101st and the British 50th Infantry Division fought northwards. This all took time, and for twenty-five hours 'Hell's Highway' was closed. It was now all but impossible to reach Urquhart. Essame's column had included several DUKW amphibious lorries filled with ammunition, which could have ferried supplies and the Poles across the river, but the Germans dominated both banks.

The continued German presence at Elst proved a distraction for Essame's 214th Brigade, which was forced to turn east to attack the town, supported by the 129th Brigade. In the meantime, 130th Brigade, under fire from Elst, headed for Driel with a dozen assault boats with which to ferry the Poles over. In the event just 200 succeeded in crossing the river to reach Oosterbeek. Horrocks's optimism had by now completely run out.

'Looking back,' recalled Horrocks, 'I am certain that this was about the bleakest moment of my life. I began to find it difficult to sleep'. On the 24th he arrived in Driel and climbed the church tower. He scanned the southern end of Urquhart's airborne bridgehead and was concerned that the paras might be cut off from the river. He resolved to put a battalion of infantry across the river to alleviate the pressure on the Oosterbeek pocket. He then hoped to left hook the 43rd Division across the river to turn the German flank. However, he knew that he simply did not have the resources to conduct such an operation.

Horrocks had not seen Field Marshal Montgomery or General Dempsey since Market Garden started. Now that the operation was at crisis point, Dempsey summoned him. An exhausted Horrocks found Dempsey, commander of the British 2nd Army, waiting for him at St Oedenrode north of Eindhoven. They discussed the realities of the situation and the prognosis was not good. Dempsey agreed that if the 43rd Division could not carry out a left hook quickly then the game was up.

When Horrocks tried to return to his headquarters north of Nijmegen he found the Germans had cut the road yet again. Rather than wait for it to be reopened, which in the event took four days, he drove cross-country with an escort. He got to his headquarters at 10 in the morning on 25 September and was informed that the 4th Dorsets had crossed the Neder Rijin during the night. This had not been a success, because thanks to German fire and the swift current many of their assault boats had been lost. There was no communication with the survivors on the far bank.

The supply situation was also hopeless: artillery ammunition had almost run out, with some guns down to five rounds each. Everything Horrocks needed, including more assault boats, was stuck to the south of the German breakthrough. Both he and General Browning concluded that Urquhart and his men would have to be withdrawn across the river before they were overrun or compelled to surrender. It was the right decision in light of 'Hell's Highway' being cut for another four days. The remnants of 1st Airborne Division could certainly not last that long.

By this stage of the war the M4 Sherman tank was woefully inadequate. In the confines of the Betuwe, the land between the Waal and Neder Rijn, Horrocks's tanks suffered at the hands of the skilful German defence. As a result the fight soon turned into an infantry battle.

The advances on Horrocks's flanks were painfully slow. The central tree bears the divisional symbol of the 53rd (Welsh) Infantry Division. The 15th (Scottish) Division, also part of the left-hand corps, struggled to maintain its bridgehead over the Meuse-Escaut Canal and suffered heavy casualties. The British 12th Corps on the right did not cross the Willems Canal until 22 September 1944.

Even above Highway 69 reconnaissance and liaison flights were not safe, as the Germans brought down a number of spotter planes.

The embankments carrying the roads in the Betuwe were exposed, leaving Horrocks's Shermans highly visible with predictable results.

Major General Thomas's 43rd Infantry Division was given the task of fighting through the Betuwe to the Polish Parachute Brigade at Driel just below the Neder Rijn. This required them to get past the German defences at Oosterhout and Elst.

This Panzer III was knocked out in Oosterhout when the British 214th Brigade attacked the village on 22 September 1944.

A Guards' Sherman in Oosterhout passing a Panzer Mk III. German armour pushing south from Elst greatly hampered Horrocks's attempts to get to Driel.

Control of Arnhem bridge enabled the Germans to feed reinforcements into the Betuwe. This included two companies of Tiger IIs from the 506th Heavy Panzer Battalion. One of these was to help with the attacks on the Oosterbeek pocket, while the second headed south into the Betuwe to help the SS at Elst.

The lead elements of the 43rd Infantry Division reached the Neder Rijn with amphibious DUKWs, but German fire dominated both banks of the river.

When German Tiger IIs got between the 43rd Division's column heading for Driel, tank-hunter teams were sent out armed with PIATs to deal with them. They destroyed three and two were abandoned.

Horrocks's dwindling supplies of ammunition meant some of his guns were reduced to five rounds each. This and the lack of fighter-bomber support meant there was little more he could do to help Urquhart's 1st Airborne Division trapped at Oosterbeek.

Chapter Eight

The Oosterbeek Pocket

By 20 September 1944 Urquhart, Hackett and Hicks (Lathbury had been wounded and captured) were trapped in the woods to the west of Oosterbeek, with their perimeter looped around the Hartenstein Hotel and anchored on the river to the south. Their situation was desperate, but the defences were holding, thanks partly to the scattered nature of the German attacks.

In getting to Oosterbeek most of Hackett's 4th Parachute Brigade was destroyed fighting its way through woods that were full of prowling German armour. These losses had finally convinced Urquhart that he simply did not have the manpower to fight his way to Arnhem bridge. Urquhart had about 3,000 men remaining, which he divided between his two brigadiers. Hicks was in charge of the western and north-western defences, while Hackett took command to the east. The tired and hungry garrison had to endure constant shelling, sniping and mortaring.

One of the most troubling German weapons was the six-barrel rocket launcher known as the Nebelwerfer. The rockets, which were pulled through the air rather than pushed, as the motor was in the front, were quite accurate and detonated before they hit the ground. British casualties increased and the divisional ammunition dump was hit. German prisoners held in the tennis courts of the Hartenstein had to be given shovels so they could dig their own trenches to shelter in.

The Germans dubbed Urquhart's last stand 'Der Kessel', or 'The Cauldron', a term they used to describe a pocket of trapped troops. Increasing numbers of German reinforcements began to arrive to bolster the 9th SS, including a battalion of Tiger IIs and a battalion of panzergrenadiers. Fortunately for the defenders, the Germans kept launching penny-packet attacks all along the perimeter, rather than concentrating their forces at one point, where they would certainly have broken through. If this had happened the defence would have been cut in two and rapidly overwhelmed. Urquhart managed to establish radio contact with 30th Corps and there was still every hope that rescue was on its way. This communication also resulted in very welcome artillery support from south of the Neder Rijn, which helped break up German infantry attacks.

Urquhart's biggest complaint was the lack of close air support. This was quite remarkable considering the role it played in Normandy. He had received none in the Arnhem area since the battle started. Urquhart should have had a 'cab rank' of fighter-bombers loitering on call, but this did not happen. Part of the problem initially was that the fighters were not permitted to operate over the battlefield when transports and gliders were flying in. This, combined with bad weather over the fighters' airfields, meant nothing was done to help. Worse still, 1st Airborne only had two ground-to-air liaison teams and they were lost to mortar fire. This was clearly another symptom of Operation Market Garden being a rushed job.

On the evening of 21 September Urquhart learned that the Poles had landed east of Driel, but this was of little help as they were on the wrong side of the river. At 2144 he signalled Browning:

> No knowledge of Div in Arnhem for 24 hours. Balance of Div in very tight perimeter. Heavy mortaring and machine-gun fire followed by local attacks. Main nuisance SP guns. Our casualties heavy. Resources stretched to utmost. Relief within 24 hours vital.

Browning knew that Urquhart could not hold out for much longer.

Nonetheless, for another four days Urquhart and his men desperately clung on. Although Field Marshal Model had ordered the destruction of 'Der Kessel', to limit their own losses his commanders were content to let the artillery do much of the dirty work. Their panzers and other armoured vehicles were very vulnerable in the close-quarter combat among the trees and ruins. However, by now most of 1st Airborne's anti-tank guns had been destroyed and PIAT ammunition had almost run out.

Finally though, with Horrocks unable to get over the river, it was decided to evacuate 1st Airborne under the cover of darkness on the night of 25/26 September. Urquhart recalled:

> The time for our going from the Hartenstein was close. The padre bade us Godspeed. We burned all our papers. In my pack I found a forgotten bottle of whisky. I handed it round; everyone in the party, I think had a nip.

On the river bank he saw his exhausted and dirty men patiently awaiting their turn to be ferried over by assault boat. Just after midnight his group departed, but their overloaded craft stuck in the mud. Urquhart's batman slipped over the side and shoved them free. The ungrateful occupants made no attempt to help him back on board, fearful they might get stuck again. Halfway across the engine died amid German machine-gun fire. Luckily it restarted and they reached the far bank and safety.

Once it was daylight it became impossible to use the boats safely. For the remaining 500 men, some of whom had acted as a rearguard to convince the Germans nothing had changed, it became a case of swim for it, evasion or surrender. Urquhart must have felt depressed when he was given the losses for his division. Of the 8,905 men who landed, along with 1,100 glider pilots, just 2,163, plus 160 Poles and 75 Dorsets, escaped 'Der Kessel' by crossing the river. Some 1,400 men had been killed and over 6,000 captured during the course of the battle.

The commander of 1st Airborne was taken to see General Browning. Urquhart, who was very tired and soaked, was not pleased to be kept waiting by Browning, who appeared looking immaculate. 'The division is nearly out now,' he said. Then added 'I am sorry we haven't been able to do what we set out to do'. Browning offered him a drink and replied 'You did all you could. Now you had better get some rest'. Urquhart also paid courtesy calls on General Horrocks and General Thomas, the commander of the 43rd Infantry Division.

The following night Browning held an ill-advised party for Urquhart and his surviving officers to celebrate the paras' rescue. While the sentiment was well intended, it was nonetheless a slightly macabre gathering. 'The dinner party was an extravagant affair for those days, with chicken and plenty of wine,' recalled an unhappy Urquhart. 'It was an ordeal even to have to face such food, let alone consume it'. He noted that Browning and Horrocks enjoyed their dinner, showing no signs of regret. Urquhart desperately wanted to ask why 30th Corps had been so badly delayed, but he never got the chance to quiz Horrocks, who as the evening wore on began to annoy him. 'It was a relief when the party ended,' said Urquhart.

He then visited Montgomery at his tactical headquarters near Eindhoven before he flew back to England. It cannot have been a meeting he particularly relished. He was greeted by banal drama. There was a bit of a panic because two of the field marshal's pet rabbits had escaped. Perhaps understandably, Urquhart was irritated by Montgomery's 'brisk radiance', and the fact that he 'did not show any disappointment' over Arnhem.

The pair discussed the battle, with Montgomery asking many questions. Montgomery claimed Urquhart asked for a message to read out to the remains of his division when he got back. Urquhart makes no mention of making such a request and stated that the following morning Montgomery emerged from his caravan 'flourishing a piece of paper'.

On 28 September 1944 Montgomery handed Urquhart a five-paragraph letter which was full praise for 1st Airborne's exemplary bravery. Key was paragraph three, which said:

In the annals of the British Army there are many glorious deeds. In our Army we have always drawn great strength and inspiration from past traditions, and endeavoured to live up to the high standards of those who have gone before. But there can be few episodes more glorious than the epic of Arnhem, and those that follow after will find it hard to live up to the standards that you have set.

Such praise was probably welcome, but many a cynical 1st Airborne survivor would have seen this as little more than Montgomery trying to put a gloss on something that had gone badly wrong. Diplomatically, Urquhart avoided commenting on what he thought of Montgomery's letter and the repeated use of the word 'glorious'.

During the eight days of Market Garden Browning's Airborne Corps lost over 11,000 casualties. This was similar to American and British losses on D-Day. American airborne casualties, including glider pilots and those of the 9th Troop Carrier Command, amounted to almost 4,000 men. Gavin's 82nd Airborne suffered 1,432 casualties and Taylor's 101st Airborne 2,118; the USAAF lost 424 aircrew and the RAF 294. On the ground Horrocks's 30th Corps suffered 1,480 casualties. Notably O'Connor's 8th and Ritchie's 12th Corps between them lost 3,874 men.

A smiling Major General Roy Urquhart in front of the Hartenstein Hotel, north-west Oosterbeek. This building was used as his divisional headquarters and would form the heart of his 'thumb-shaped' Oosterbeek defensive perimeter once Arnhem bridge was lost. It was not far from the Tafelberg Hotel, where Field Marshal Model was having lunch on 17 September 1944 when the paras first landed.

Men of 1st Airborne near the Hartenstein on 20 September. It was to this point in the British perimeter that the 156th Parachute Battalion conducted a successful fighting withdrawal. The battalion was then deployed south of Oosterbeek railway station.

Airborne 75mm Pack Howitzer defending the Oosterbeek pocket. These weapons proved invaluable. They could fire high explosive (HE) rounds out to 8,660 metres at a rate of six rounds per minute. Fire support was also provided by the OML 2in, 3in and 4.2in mortars, which could also fire HE and smoke.

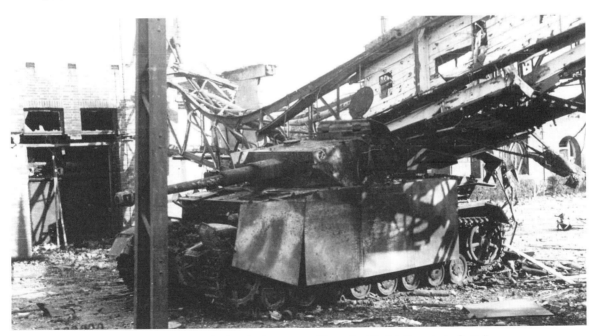

German Panzer IV knocked out in the Arnhem area. Once Frost's 1st Parachute Battalion had been overcome, the Germans were able to concentrate their forces against Urquhart.

SdKfz 250 half-track belonging to Harzer's 9th SS probing 1st Airborne's defences at Oosterbeek. Note the parachute draped over the bushes in the background.

The Oosterbeek 'Der Kessel' was pounded by German rocket launchers. This captured example is a heavy calibre 280/320mm Nebelwerfer 41. Its 280mm HE rockets had a range of about 2,000 metres.

1st Airborne trenches in the woods around Oosterbeek. These men are armed with the Mk V Sten gun, which was fitted with a solid wooden butt, which replaced the metal triangular tube stocks fitted to the earlier models.

A classic and much-reproduced image of British paras at Oosterbeek. Although probably posed, it does capture the fighting spirit of the 1st Airborne Division.

A British para using the American-supplied M1 carbine. A version with folding stock was designed for airborne use.

Exhausted-looking 1st Airborne prisoners being marched through Oosterbeek. Under the cover of darkness on the night of 25 September 1944 just 2,400 members of the division were evacuated back over the Neder Rijn. Of the 10,000 men who had gone into battle, 1,400 were killed and over 6,000 captured.

Prisoners being rounded up outside the Vreewijk Hotel to the east of the Hartenstein. This was on the Utrechtseweg road and on the right flank of Urquhart's defensive perimeter. There was simply not time to evacuate everyone, as a daylight river crossing was impossible with the Germans controlling both banks – some 500 men remained in Oosterbeek.

An abandoned Tiger II. Fortunately for 30th Corps and 1st Airborne the German crews proved to be inexperienced and did not press home their attacks with any great vigour. However, their presence, along with the SS, still played a part in thwarting Market Garden.

Chapter Nine

Arnhem Liberated

Operation Market Garden brought false hope to the Netherlands. North of the Neder Rijn and elsewhere, the Dutch were not to be freed from Nazi occupation by the end of 1944 as they had fervently hoped. Instead they had to endure another winter, with many of them running desperately short of food. Following the evacuation of the 1st Airborne Division the city of Arnhem was not liberated until over six months later by the British Army in mid-April 1945, with the arrival of the 45th (West Riding) Infantry Division.

With the benefit of hindsight Operation Market Garden is full of 'what ifs' – none of them particularly helpful. The reality is that instead of holding out for two to four days, the unfortunate 1st Airborne Division remained trapped for over a week, lost control of Arnhem bridge and was driven back across the river with heavy losses. After the war Major General Urquhart – publicly at least – showed no bitterness over what had happened to the 1st Airborne. In his account of the battle he wrote 'The lack of intelligence was a nuisance, but hardly more than that'. This was generous to say the least.

'The handicap of the division being landed in three lifts was one from which we never recovered,' he said in his official report. There was no getting away from the fact that the division's four brigades had been unable to act in unison. Crucially, on the first day 1st Parachute Brigade had been on its own. Urquhart was critical of the decision not to land south of the river so as to secure the bridges from both ends, and of letting German flak shape their landing plans.

He also pointed out that his paras were not adequately prepared for the bitter street-fighting. The focus had always been getting to the bridge, not urban warfare. The German response had likewise been unhelpful:

> The speed and efficiency of the German reaction was impressive: the German soldier has always been trained in immediate counter-attack and this was shown in the early days at Arnhem.

Montgomery and Dempsey should have been alert to this danger – if they were, they chose to ignore it. Urquhart bemoaned the lack of close air support, saying that it was a 'surprise'. He concluded 'whatever the reasons, fighter support was not forthcoming except in small numbers and very late in the battle'.

It has been alleged that a member of the Dutch resistance betrayed Market Garden to German intelligence. Just two days before the operation commenced the Germans were informed that an attack was anticipated toward Eindhoven, but as the British were already pressing in this direction it was hardly news. Also the information made no reference to Arnhem. Urquhart pointed to the fact that Field Marshal Model only just escaped from Oosterbeek as sufficient evidence that the Germans were genuinely caught by surprise. The presence of the SS was just bad luck rather than deliberate.

Frost was rightly proud of his men's achievements. They had resisted to the last. 'No body of men could have fought more courageously and tenaciously,' he said, 'than the officers and men of the 1st Parachute Brigade'.

Montgomery remained unapologetic for the failure of Market Garden, although he accepted that Urquhart's men were dropped too far from Arnhem bridge, saying 'I take the blame for this mistake'. Regarding the presence of the 2nd SS Corps, he acknowledged 'We knew it was there. But we were wrong in supposing that it could not fight effectively; its battle state was far beyond our expectation'. Ultimately Montgomery held Eisenhower responsible for not backing him with sufficient resources to carry the day.

Montgomery steadfastly refused to accept that withholding intelligence on the SS contributed to both Urquhart and Horrocks being thwarted in attaining their goals. He concluded, almost with an air of complacency:

> In my prejudiced view, if the operation had been properly backed from its inception, and given the aircraft, ground forces, and administrative resources necessary for the job – it would have succeeded *in spite* of my mistakes, or the adverse weather, or the presence of the 2nd SS Panzer Corps in the Arnhem area. I remain Market Garden's unrepentant advocate.

In other words, he claimed the failure was not his fault. Perhaps he could have been humbler, but that was not Montgomery's way. There is an English saying that 'a bad craftsman blames his tools'. The plan was Montgomery's, no one else's. To blame Horrocks would be a gross injustice.

Montgomery's astute chief of staff, General de Guingand, agreed with Urquhart, listing three reasons for the operation's failure. These were insufficient air lift, the bad weather and the strength of the enemy's response. The weather in war is always a gamble despite the meteorologists, though the Allies had hoped that it would be better than it was. De Guingand noted with understatement 'I think we had perhaps underestimated the enemy's power of recuperation'.

De Guingand, like so many senior officers, tried to put a gloss on things, highlighting that 30th Corps had liberated a large area of the Netherlands and that Nijmegen bridge was to prove of immense value later. Nonetheless, he acknowledged that:

> it is only fair to recall that the primary objective was to gain possession of the area between Arnhem and the Zuider Zee, preparatory to crossing the Issel River into Northern Germany. In this we failed.

Horrocks rather unfairly shouldered the blame, saying:

> The main criticism has always been that 30th Corps was very slow. If this is so, it was my fault because all the troops were imbued with a sense of desperate urgency.

His main regret was that he had attempted to push direct from Nijmegen to Arnhem. Instead, he wished he had crossed the Waal farther to the west of Nijmegen. This would have enabled a left hook toward the western edge of the airborne perimeter. Nevertheless, he was firmly of the view that even if he had got over the Neder Rijn, they would have never reached the Zuider Zee.

In his memoirs, Horrocks wrote that Operation Market Garden was simply too ambitious:

> Even if the 2nd German SS Panzer Corps had not been in a position to intervene so rapidly, and if we had succeeded in getting right through to the Zuider Zee, could we have kept our long lines of communication open? I very much doubt it. In which case, instead of 30th Corps fighting to relieve the 1st British Airborne Division, it would have been a case of the remainder of the 2nd Army struggling desperately to relieve 30th Corps cut off by the Germans north of Arnhem. Maybe in the long run we were lucky.

He summed up:

> Perhaps I can best conclude by saying that any great military operation is considerably affected by unpredictable events. Whereas almost everything had fallen in our favour and gone according to plan during the Normandy landings, Arnhem was just the reverse; nothing seemed to go right.

The British have a habit of making defeat look rather glorious. 'Few, if any, of those who stood at Arnhem Bridge in 1944,' said Lieutenant Colonel Frost, 'can have imagined that their lonely battle would ever become so famous'. Ironically, had Horrocks reached them it would probably not have achieved the status that it did. Instead Cornelius Ryan turned it into an iconic battle – known aptly as *A Bridge too Far*.

Damaged buildings being demolished in Arnhem. Frost's heroic defence of the bridge had been for nothing – after the defeat of 1st Airborne the town remained occupied by the Germans until the spring of 1945.

General Gavin's 82nd Airborne did everything they could to help 30th Corps, as did the 101st, but German resistance at Nijmegen, the Betuwe and at Arnhem ultimately thwarted Market Garden.

General Gavin being decorated by Field Marshal Montgomery, who awarded him the British Distinguished Service Order on 21 March 1945. Montgomery refused to acknowledge that Market Garden was flawed from the start and preferred to blame Eisenhower for his defeat.

A crashed RAF Hawker Typhoon Mk IB fighter-bomber. One of General Urquhart's complaints after the battle was the paucity of close air support he received at Arnhem. The weather was held to blame, but this was not the whole story.

This Tiger II was knocked out on the last day of battle at Oosterbeek. The paras used the remains of their ammunition for a 6-pounder and 75mm gun plus a PIAT to destroy the tank. The heavy Tiger II was designed as a breakthrough weapon, not for urban warfare. The crew would have little idea where danger lurked among the ruined buildings.

Dutch civilians welcome a British Sherman crew. Many of the Dutch people would have to endure another miserable winter under the Nazi yoke.

An American anti-tank gun crew under fire somewhere in the Netherlands in early November 1944.

The Americans first crossed the Rhine at Remagen in early March 1945 after capturing a railway bridge.

An American M5 light tank on the streets in Germany.

British infantry advancing through Arnhem, supported by a Humber scout car, on 14 April 1945. This time they were not thrown out.

Once again the town suffered damage while the remaining Germans were evicted. The crew of this Sherman Crab flail tank keeps a look out for snipers while watching a nearby blazing building.

Arnhem was liberated by units including elements of the 49th (West Riding) Infantry Division. The cheering crowds knew they were here to stay.

These carriers belonging to the 49th Division were given a very warm welcome by the locals.

A re-creation of the SS rolling over Arnhem road bridge staged for the movie *A Bridge Too Far*, on which John Frost acted as a technical advisor. The accuracy of the vehicles leaves a lot to be desired. This film was to become mired in controversy over actor Dirk Bogarde's portrayal of General Browning.

Movie Controversy

While Cornelius Ryan's book has stood the test of time, the movie is another matter. Director Richard Attenborough had his hands full with an international A-lister cast who did not make his job any easier. Major General John Frost (at the time of Arnhem a lieutenant colonel), although an advisor on *A Bridge Too Far*, was not a big fan of the finished movie. Despite the reliable hand of Attenborough, the resulting film was rather incoherent and Frost disliked some of the deliberate artistic licence. Also, Frost's presence for the filming of the Arnhem bridge sequences did not make actor Anthony Hopkins' (who portrayed Frost) job any easier. They reportedly disliked each other from the very start.

There was far greater controversy than this. The movie, intentionally or otherwise, made General 'Boy' Browning look an uncaring villain. Actor Dirk Bogarde got into trouble for his rather fey portrayal of Browning, which led to vigorous complaints from Browning's widow, the novelist Daphne du Maurier. Bogarde was very upset by the backlash.

> There were cries of fury and distress from the widow and the family of the man I was representing, and anger was expressed, so I was reliably informed, from Windsor Castle to Clarence House.

During the war Bogarde, as a young officer, had served in Europe as an air photographic interpreter attached to 39 Wing of the Canadian Royal Air Force. He witnessed the agony of Arnhem, remarking:

> We had no need of the books the generals might later write to explain things. We saw it happen before our eyes, unwilling witnesses to a shattering disaster.

Seconded to an infantry division, he spent the winter on the south side of the river while the Dutch starved. He went on to say in his defence:

> I didn't see the film, so I am not qualified to make any comment, nor can I judge where, or if, I went wrong. I had known the officer I played, in Normandy and in Holland: the very last thing I would have dreamed of doing was to defame his character or reputation, but both of which I was told I had; God knows how.

Maybe deep down Bogarde had some personal agenda with his portrayal of Browning, but it seems unlikely. Perhaps his crime was simply to be too 'method' in his approach.

Furthermore, Bogarde did not get on with fellow actor Sean Connery, who played General Urquhart. It took a day to shoot their scene together and there was a tense atmosphere, which ironically probably helped inform their performances. Afterwards Bogarde retreated to his house in the south of France to devote his energies to writing his hugely successful autobiographies and novels. The movie was not a commercial or critical success, but has since inspired successive generations of Arnhem historians and remains a valiant attempt to capture the drama of Operation Market Garden.

Further Reading

Antony Beevor, *Arnhem: The Battle for the Bridges, 1944*. London: Viking, 2018

David Bennett, *A Magnificent Disaster: The Failure of Market Garden, the Arnhem Operation, September 1944*. Philadelphia: Casemate, 2008

William F. Buckingham, *Arnhem 1944: A Reappraisal*. Stroud: Tempus, 2002

Major General John Frost, *A Drop Too Many*. London: Cassell, 1980/Barnsley: Pen & Sword, 2009

Louis Hagen, *Arnhem Lift*. London: Leo Cooper, 1993

Martin Middlebrook, *Arnhem 1944: The Airborne Battle*. London: Viking, 1994/Barnsley: Pen & Sword, 2017

Alexander Morrison, *Silent Invader: A Glider Pilot's Story of the Invasion of Europe in World War II*. Shrewsbury: Airlife, 1999/2002

John Nichol & Tony Rennell, *Arnhem: The Battle for Survival*. London: Viking, 2011/London: Penguin, 2012

Geoffrey Powell, *The Devil's Birthday: The Bridges to Arnhem, 1944*. London: Buchan & Enright, 1984

Cornelius Ryan, *A Bridge Too Far*. London: Hamish Hamilton, 1974

Tim Saunders, *Nijmegen: US 82nd Airborne and Guards Armoured Division*. Barnsley: Leo Cooper, 2001

Major General R.R. Urquhart, CB, DSO, *Arnhem*. London: Cassell, 1958/London: Pan, 1972